BAUDELAIRE

BAUDELAIRE:

THE PARADOX OF REDEMPTIVE SATANISM

Pierre Emmanuel

Translated
by
Robert T. Cargo

The University of Alabama Press
University, Alabama

Translated into English from *Baudelaire*, Copyright © 1967
by Desclée De Brouwer
English translation copyright © 1970
by The University of Alabama Press
Standard Book Number: 8173-7602-x
Library of Congress Catalog Card Number: 78-104929
All rights reserved
Manufactured in the United States of America

Table of Contents

Translator's Preface

It would be safe to say without qualification, I believe, that Baudelaire is in our day the best known French poet both in his native land and abroad. This widespread interest in his work, together with the exceptional perspicacity of Pierre Emmanuel's critical appraisal of the quality of Baudelaire's religious experience, has convinced me of the desirability of making Emmanuel's study available to those English-speaking readers for whom it might otherwise be inaccessible.

The question of Baudelaire's religion, while being certainly one of the fundamental problems pertaining to the author of *Les Fleurs du Mal,* is the one about which there is the most significant and serious disagreement. In the past, all too often, Catholic writers have almost forcibly declared the poet to be one of their own, disregarding many a text where Baudelaire seems to cry out in vain protest. Less sympathetic writers, on the other hand, have chosen to emphasize the satanic elements in his writings to the point where they deny that one can justifiably call Baudelaire Catholic or even Christian.

Pierre Emmanuel, one of France's leading Catholic poets and literary critics, brings what I believe to be a heretofore unequaled competence to bear on this particular aspect of Baudelaire. A poet's sensitivity and intuition, a masterful understanding of the complexities of craft, the sure, rigorous method of the mature critic are combined with an equally rigorous theology and psychology. The result is a study that looks at Baudelaire in the broad pattern of Christian tradition but with careful attention being paid likewise to the poet's spiritual aspirations as seen in terms of aesthetics and artistic creation.

I wish to acknowledge my indebtedness to some whose work I have found helpful. I have made considerable use of William Aggeler's very fine translation of *Les Fleurs du Mal* (Fresno: Academy Library Guild, 1954). Only infrequently has it been necessary to introduce some slight variations so as to make the translated passage reflect more clearly a particular aspect that the writer in citing from Baudelaire's verse wished to emphasize. Likewise, I have found useful the more recent translations by Jonathan Mayne from Baudelaire's critical writings, *Baudelaire. The Painter of Modern Life and Other Exhibitions* (London: Phaidon Press, 1964) and *Baudelaire. Art in Paris 1845–1862: Salons and Other Exhibitions,* published by the same press in 1965. These volumes, together with Enid Starkie's biography of the poet, *Baudelaire* (New York: New Directions, 1957), will serve to guide those readers who may feel that some introductory reading is necessary.

Citations from Baudelaire are identified by the writer in the text proper. The notes throughout the volume are those of the translator.

Robert T. Cargo

University, Alabama
October, 1969

Chronology

1821   Charles Pierre Baudelaire is born (April 9) in Paris.

1827   His father, Joseph-François Baudelaire, dies (February 10).

1828   His mother, Caroline Archenbaut-Defayis Baudelaire, marries Captain (later Commandant) Jacques Aupick (November 8).

1831 Years of study—first in Lyon, then at the Lycée Louis-le-
to   Grand and the Lévêque and Bailly Pension—leading to a
1839 *baccalauréat* degree.

1840   Baudelaire has his first literary contacts: Gérard de Nerval, Balzac.

1841 He travels to Ile Maurice and Ile Bourbon, at the urging of
to   Aupick, who hopes to separate Baudelaire from bad influ-
1842 ences in Paris.

1842   Baudelaire meets Gautier and Théodore de Banville. He forms a liaison with Jeanne Duval, a second-rate, mulatto actress (the Black Venus).*

---

*Poems xxii–xxxix, as well as *Les Bijoux, Le Léthé,* and perhaps *Chanson d'Après-midi,* in *Les Fleurs du Mal* were inspired by Jeanne Duval [trans. note].

1843 He moves to the Hôtel Pimodan. First debts.

1844 Narcisse-Désiré Ancelle is appointed Baudelaire's legal guardian, at his mother's request.

1845 Publication of the first two *Salons*. On June 30, 1845, attempt at suicide.

1847 Appearance of *La Fanfarlo,* a story imitated from Balzac.

1848 Baudelaire takes part in the Revolution, including worker riots of June. He breaks off his relations with his mother over Jeanne Duval.

1851 Discovery of Joseph de Maistre and Edgar Allan Poe. First
to   anonymous letter to Madame Sabatier (the White
1852 Venus),* with whom Baudelaire forms a strange liaison, seeing her socially while courting her anonymously by correspondence.

1853 Years of misery. Succession of anonymous letters to Ma-
to   dame Sabatier. Publication of the first translations from
1856 Poe, serialized in *Le Pays*. Article on psychology of laughter, *L'Essence du Rire*. June 1, 1855: *La Revue des Deux Mondes* publishes eighteen poems of Baudelaire under the title, *Les Fleurs du Mal*.

1857 Death of General Aupick. June 25: The first edition of *Les Fleurs du Mal,* containing one hundred poems, goes on sale. July 16: the work is seized by the authorities. August 18: Baudelaire reveals his identity to Madame Sabatier. August 20: Baudelaire and his publisher are ordered by the courts to pay fines and to delete six poems from the

* Poems XL–XLVIII constitute the Madame Sabatier cycle [trans. note].

work. August 31: the affair with Madame Sabatier is ended. [Baudelaire's third serious liaison, with the actress Marie Daubrun (the Green-Eyed Venus),* spanning the decade from 1850–1860, was rather sporadic and coincided somewhat with the Madame Sabatier affair.]

1858 Baudelaire suffers his first serious illness. He considers living with his mother in Honfleur, but decides against it. In Paris with no permanent address, he resides with Jeanne Duval.

1859 Jeanne is stricken with paralysis. Baudelaire rents a little
to apartment in Neuilly and lives there with her. The work
1860 on drugs, *Les Paradis artificiels*, is published.

1861 Baudelaire suffers new and morbid symptoms. The second edition of *Les Fleurs du Mal* appears with thirty-five new poems added;** and "Richard Wagner et Tannhäuser" is published in the *Revue Européenne*. Baudelaire seeks admission to the Académie Française.

1862 Baudelaire receives a "strange warning" of his inner troubles. He abandons his attempts to gain election to the Académie. His half brother, Claude-Alphonse (by the first wife of Baudelaire's father), dies following a cerebral hemorrhage complicated by hemiplegia. The first of the *poèmes en prose* appears.

1863 Delacroix dies, and Baudelaire publishes a necrological article on the painter in *Opinion nationale*. His study of

* Poems XLIX–LVII were written for Marie Daubrun [trans. note].
** This edition of 1861, being the last to appear during Baudelaire's lifetime, is therefore considered to be the definitive edition. Had Baudelaire lived, in all probability he would have incorporated at least some of those poems added to the posthumous third edition [trans. note].

Constantin Guys, *Peintre de la Vie moderne,* also appears during the year.

1864 Baudelaire travels in Belgium. His lecture series fails, and
to it is generally a year of aggravation and increasing discom-
1865 fort. *Pauvre Belgique!* is composed. Baudelaire spends a brief period in Paris to obtain money and returns to Brussels. Mallarmé and Verlaine publish enthusiastic articles on Baudelaire, who remarks, "These young fellows scare the life out of me."

1866 Still in Belgium, Baudelaire suffers dizziness and nausea and, on March 6,* paralysis of the right side of his body; he is hospitalized in Brussels. In July he is brought back to Paris by his mother and treated in the clinic of Dr. Duval.

1867 Death brings an end to months of suffering, at 11:00 A.M. on August 31.

* Or at least sometime during this month, probably between March 5 and March 22 [trans. note].

BAUDELAIRE

Abbreviations

In referring to works by Baudelaire, the author has used the following abbreviations:

A.R.	*Art Romantique* (1868–69)
C.E.	*Curiosités Esthétiques* (1868–69)
F.M.	*Fleurs du Mal* (1857)
H.E.	*Histoires Extraordinaires*
N.H.E.	*Nouvelles Histoires Extraordinaires*
J.I.	*Journaux Intimes* (1887)
Œ.P.	*Œuvres Posthumes*
P.A.	*Les Paradis Artificiels* (1860)
P.P.P.	*Petits Poèmes en Prose* (1869)

I. The Archetype

"It tempts the partisan critic, even now, to adopt Baudelaire as the patron of his own beliefs." Written in 1930, this statement by Eliot is still true.[1] More than Rimbaud, Baudelaire has become a myth: "the greatest exemplar in *modern* poetry in any language," says Eliot in the same essay. The myth is that of the poetic absolute: verbal allurement or divine milieu? What is there behind the "sacred" terminology of the poet? An art of self-esteem or a faith? Psychological "faith," or religious adherence? Involutive immanence, illusionary transcendance; or spiritual tropism, recourse to the Unique? Does the poetic word suffer or not from an irreducible ambivalence? For commentators, this is the fundamental question. Catholic exegetes of Baudelaire make a Christian of him, albeit a faithless one. For reasons just as partial, and sometimes contradictory, some who are not Catholic deny that he is. A third category of critics, often poets and his descendants, see him as an aesthetic Christian—Christian in his themes but without being so before God.

At the time Eliot was writing, the tendency in criticism was to look upon Baudelaire as a "Christian, Catholic and serious." Eliot shared this view, though with "considerable reservation." Baudelaire's Christianity appeared to him to be "rudimentary, embryonic." His satanism, on the other hand, in Eliot's opinion, was "an attempt to get into Christianity by the back door" and was thus "redeemed by meaning something else." This something else is "the possibility of damnation," and, therefore, also of personal salvation: "so immense a relief" in the middle of a gregarious and scientific nineteenth century, for which *progress* and *reaction* replace good and evil. For according to Eliot, Baudelaire gives primary importance precisely to "the real problem of good and evil"; that is to say, to sin and redemption, understood "in the permanent Christian sense."

"*Poeta christianissimus*" Rudolf Kassner calls him; Baudelaire is also that for Charles du Bos, whether he adheres to dogma or not. A man can cease to believe without ceasing to be Christian. Du Bos goes so far as to suggest that in Baudelaire the loss of faith could be only an appearance due to "conditions and [. . .] almost superhuman exigences willed by him in the notion and in the act of faith." Besides—and psychologically this is the essential thing—the loss of faith "does not carry with it in all individuals the disappearance of the notion of sin, quite to the contrary; and deprived henceforth of the counterbalance that belief and especially Christian practice provide, this idea of sin imbeds itself in one's soul only to torment it." Barbey d'Aurevilly was the first to see this; soon after the appearance of *Les Fleurs du Mal* he called attention to the "cries of a Christian soul, made ill by the infinite." Thinking perhaps of *Une Martyre,* Barbey calls Baudelaire "a Rancé without faith."[2] To this "great poet who does not believe himself to be Christian and who, in his book, positively does not want to be," he brutally offers as an alternative: "either to blow his brains out . . . or become a Christian!" On the other hand, for Stanislas Fumet, Baudelaire has chosen, or has been chosen: "he is in the hands of the Creator and he has not wandered into the labyrinth without being provided with the notion of original Sin, which is the lamp of Catholicism." It remains to be seen whether this lamp merely reveals the walls of the aesthetic cavern, or whether it illuminates the conscience in search of God. Léon Daudet does not hesitate to situate Baudelaire's fight against himself at Calvary, which, he thinks, haunts the poet's life and work. In this struggle, Baudelaire's "powerful and brilliant" reason "has depended on the cross in the most dramatic fashion, like Pascal's. One cannot say that it won. Neither can one say that it lost." And Daudet is not afraid to write that, faced with "a person of this stature, there always comes a time when criticism must yield to theology."

Jean-Pierre Richard does not accept this change of scheme either in the critics or in the poet, who is the first exegete of his existence "in terms of ideology, of theology." Resolutely drawn by the only perceptible beauty, formal perfection, Richard identifies its felicitous expression with the joy of creation, and shows Baudelaire to be a happy artist. As if Baudelaire had planned his neurosis in view of this particular happiness, the critic takes pleasure in revealing the forbidden will, the "salutary power" of which Baudelaire was unaware in his art, and which *transmuted his suffering into his work*. With the man and his misfortune annihilated, art alone, pure in its essence, remains: the imagination changes the psychic abyss woefully explored by Baudelaire into theater and scenery. About this art, if not about the man who produced it, Jean-Pierre Richard can thus say that "fundamentally it preserves well its magic, its sacred verticality, its power of resonance and vertigo, but he empties it also of its terrors, since he himself ends on a semantic plane, in a precise and completely human sense." In other words, on the psychic canvas, art would produce effects of "absolute" perspective: the transcendant would be only a game for the soul. In his efforts to eliminate the role of God from Baudelaire's work, Richard pushes subtlety to the point of citing this name only twice, in reference to the sun of which he makes the true word incarnate according to Baudelaire. "Everything happens [in *Élévation*]as if the sun itself had deigned to leave its inaccessible zenith, as if it had come down to drown itself in the realm of men, to fill it with its warmth and stir it with its fecundity. From this point, there is no longer any need to pursue transcendence, 'the God who withdraws,' into the ultimate depths. . . ."

No less brilliantly than Richard, Sartre analyzes the distances that he considers to be faked, the perspectives reputed to be false. Where the critic admires the artifice of beauty, the philosopher unmasks the mechanism of failure. On Baudelaire's "religion," he cites an opinion of Jules Lemaître: "Because nothing equals religious sentiments in intensity and in depth (because of the terror and love they may contain) we seize upon them, we rekindle them within ourselves—and this, in earnest search of sensations which are the most directly condemned by the beliefs from which these sentiments derive. We thus arrive at something wonderfully artificial. . . ." If the artist in Baudelaire finds Beauty, or more precisely *his Beauty,* it is because Baudelaire the man, such as Sartre *conceives* him, seeks punishment, makes himself automatically guilty. Moreover, and still according to Sartre, Baudelaire believes too little in God to fear hell. Another "whip-wielding father" makes him tremble, and this one is quite real, General Aupick.[3] And Sartre asserts peremptorily: "Baudelaire, we have seen, never had faith except at such time when he was weakened by illness."

Such is also, in quite a different system, the conviction of Yves Bonnefoy: "Baudelaire neither spoke of nor experienced any faith." He perceives in the poet, however, "an anger, a resentment concerning too strong a religion, one that grew in his work to the point of changing the meaning of it." A meaning which is not God, but death. "He invented, when God for many had ceased to be, the idea that death can be efficacious, that it

alone will reform the unity of lost man." Here Bonnefoy, draw-
ing from an apophatic art, gives us in Baudelaire his own idea of
reintegration with essence. "It [death] would accomplish the
destiny of the word. It would open the abode of poetry to
religious sentiment, at the end of its long wandering." This is an
attitude which is analogous to the "sacral" aesthetic of Jean-
Pierre Richard, whose criticism is a treatise on poetry rather than
an analysis. The ambiguous spirituality of the artist creates by
itself its "religion," which recovers the values of the former faith,
including grandeur of evil. "In a society which detests the eternal," writes Bonnefoy, "Baudelaire loved evil like an outburst of
the absolute." Pierre Jean Jouve, in whom poetic and religious
ambivalence is no less great, sees in this evil an "enormous
suffering" and the Daudelairian way toward essence, "with which
he is enamoured." The one he apostrophizes by this verse: "O
beloved O magnificent O very holy saint Baudelaire . . . ," is
really for him, through the sense of original sin, this *vir christianissimus* through whom, "from the dark depths to the light,
passes the continuous current of a spiritual will, of a haggard and
infinitely touching search for God." The same Baudelaire in
whom a Bonnefoy would see the first great post-Christian spiritual figure remains for Jouve—without being contradictory—a
"spiritual poet of Christian stock," whose "virtue of suffering is
that of Christianity," but whose God is the "God of Christians
who no longer belong to any church." The word *spiritual*, which
comes up frequently in Jouve and Bonnefoy, masks a mysticism
that they neither identify nor distinguish from mystique. Benjamin Fondane is more direct: "The hatred that he [Baudelaire]
has for himself is not only philosophical, it is *holy: aborreci-
miento santo de si mismo* [the sacred abhorrence of one's own
self]—exactly as in the case of Saint John of the Cross. To con-
quer and deny the self—salvation comes at this price! In his ide-
alistic passion, he brings *also* the medieval, Dantesque, Catholic,

mystical passion; good and evil still have for him a substance, a tangible quality, a concreteness; the void that he seeks is not a pure void, but 'shadows'. . . ."

We sense in poetry and critics of poetry today the temptation to such hyperbole, which makes a mystique of poetry and a holy word of the poem. Their tendency is to substitute an immanent religiosity, self-sufficient because it is self-creative, for faith in the Transcendent and particularly for Christian faith. Modern poets have pushed mimesis of the sacred to the extreme. It is seen in certain approaches to Baudelaire; it is true that there have been some Christian critics who have contributed to the confusion. But on the question of Baudelaire's *christianity* and not his religious imagination, some who have analyzed the work have made reservations and distinctions that are fitting and proper. Max Milner notes the essential fact that Christ the redeemer is absent from the work, thus upsetting the balance on the side of evil. Another capital remark: Baudelaire speaks a great deal about original sin, but his concept of it is not a Christian one; it is the creation itself that he considers to be bad and that he looks upon sometimes as "the fall of God." Georges Blin thinks that this fall, and the duality that it introduces, was for Baudelaire only an appearance, and that in any case the emanatistic theory of this notion is in contradiction with the Christian idea of a personal God. The idea of the Redemption is lacking in Baudelaire, as Daniel Vouga in turn points out, "unless one accepts, along with certain commentators who are too zealous or too easily satisfied, the idea that to believe in the Fall is of necessity to believe in the Redemption, and that to believe in Sin is of necessity to believe in Grace."

In the examination of these fundamental concepts, here ambiguous, we come upon the intuitions of Paul Arnold, who relates Baudelaire's cosmogony to Pythagorism and to neo-Platonism, perhaps to ancient Asia. Arnold denies to Baudelaire "the Christian position, indeed even such an orientation." Baudelaire does not seek to "surmount the irreversibility" of the fall; "he knows that by its presence in matter, the human soul risks [. . .] continuing to corrupt itself, in other words uniting itself ever more intimately with matter—which is its own initial desire infinitely enlarged." Thus the only conceivable spirituality for the poet would be, in the heart of corruption, a vigilance of a well defined nature: "hyperconsciousness in evil which detaches to some degree the soul from terrestrial works."

This brief contradictory criticism of the great "religious" themes in Baudelaire opens, in the guise of justification, the exegesis which follows. As those which have preceded it, this exegesis will be incomplete and biased in two respects: it will accept many suggestions, but it will arrive at their implications by different ways. My guiding idea is simple. The greater a poet is, the more his own life—whatever it may be made up of—thrusts itself upon him like the source of a universal enigma. In endeavoring to express this enigma, he gives depth to it, and to his *concrete* existence with it, in a manner that literally *splits asunder*. A privileged subject of contradiction, the poet is thus the witness of an irreducible suffering that he *cultivates,* to the extent of malady and fault, like the instrument of concealed knowledge. Every poetic life is filled with sorrow and pain and suffering: its vision of unity comes at this price. The debate with God— whether he exists or not for the poet—imposes itself in the flesh as much as in the work. When consciousness is on a par with the suffering, as in a Baudelaire whose entire body of work is a reflection on his destiny and on the act of creating, God is no longer, not to any degree at all, one literary theme among others: He is present, without being named as such, in the very fabric of the work and in the exigence that the poet takes on trust, weak creature that he is and precisely because he is so. The formation of the idea of God is identified with that of one's self: it is the genesis of a relation. To study, if not "Baudelaire and his relation to God," at least the religiosity of Baudelaire, is to trace his spiritual development from the germ imbedded in his psychic being, taking into consideration the great accidents of his nature and of his life. From these events, Baudelaire's idiosyncrasy nourished the myth that he made of himself for himself, and which he calls his *fate*. Another finality, both transcendent and personal, gives them order in my opinion: the intention, the action of God upon this man—intention, action hidden *in* and often masked *by* the action of this man upon his own secret. Ambivalent from man's viewpoint, the relation is *one* as seen by God.

This man struggles, often against God, to attain the freedom that surrounds them, both God and him; and God works in man by this very freedom. While forcing myself not to bypass even a single step of the poet in the approach to these realities or to these dreams, to these psychic concretions or to these truths of a spiritual order that he names *sin, evil, religion, God,* I propose in principle, because I believe it, that Baudelaire walks facing a supreme Reality and toward it, and that *the aesthetic way has a meaning, were it only to end contradictorily in an impasse, although within sight of Reality.* Perhaps I shall be accused of having descended quite deep into the poet's soul in order to fix there the origin of this path. It is the depth to which I would descend within myself, in view of such an end. That the spiritual can be born thus from the carnal appears to me to be the work of incarnation, slow, obscure, but wonderful. *God is born in us* in the same way as we come into the world, and he grows in the conditions in which we grow, constrained by them but using them to invent in us our loftiest freedom. The neurotic elements of individuality can become organs of spiritual perception in the service of the person. Inversely, the tension of a superior mind can exhaust the psychic part of the being and can produce

accidents analogous to neurosis. Those are risks to take in view of
an end which is not derived from mere natural disposition but
which is often the sign of the contradiction that reveals it.
That is why the first two chapters of this book, apparently
consecrated to the psychism of Baudelaire in its most visceral
aspects, are a necessary gestation for the birth of the subject
treated here, for the birth of God in the poet. Had I omitted this
gestation, I would have reduced God to a concept cut off from its
genesis. Now what interested me was not only the idea of God
that Baudelaire formed but, above all, the germination of God in
Baudelaire's being.

To this preliminary confession of the limits of my objectivity I
add a note of precision on my feelings with respect to the poet of
Les Fleurs du Mal. I formerly wrote, in an issue of the *Revue des
Sciences Humaines*[4] devoted to Baudelaire, a text that the following study will invalidate in part. A year of rigorous familiarity
with the work of the poet has separated me further than ever
from a "heresy" whose father he once appeared to me to be: that
of poetry as spiritual salvation. But this familiarity has likewise
convinced me of the exemplary nature of his poetic destiny. It is
the aim of this book to show in what way he is exemplary.

II. Erotic Religion

1. The Unitive Life

From earliest childhood, perhaps even in the mother's womb, are formed the directive lines of a destiny. The adult who attempts to break these determinants or to free himself in them, reacts by constituting himself in relation to this fatality, to this initial basic idea. We apply the word *unconscious* to this vague, shadowy memory, which, when we fail to control it, we likewise call forgetfulness: the past anterior of our consciousness, of our very existences, and the yet active present in us; affective substratum, barely or not at all elucidated, of a dialogue which we pursue with our being, with our senses, at depths which escape us by their evidence or their obscurity.

Sarte observes that we must "discover, in relationship with the past, the essence of what we call the Baudelairian *poetic deed.*" He generalizes upon this idea: "Each poet pursues in his own fashion this synthesis of existence and being that we have recognized for an impossibility." Thus, by the a priori of the system, all efficaciousness of the poet's function is denied. We know what being is for Sartre: "the mode of stubborn and rigorously defined presence of an object"; this past, with which Baudelaire would like to identify himself, would be the ensemble of things and moments of childhood, fixed, immobilized once and for all in an enchanted light. And existence would be the contrary: rupture, forward movement, creation of the pure new; to *being* would be opposed *doing*. Of course, if being and existence were as Sartre understands them, radically separated, if the freedom of the individual did not participate in eternal creation, the poetic endeavor would be a chimera. It would be so if the Sartrian postulate were true that consciousness, in Baudelaire as in anyone, "is seized first of all in its entire gratuity, without cause and without aim, amorphous, unjustifiable, having no other claim to existence than the fact that it exists already." Too trenchant, too slick a formula: Baudelaire, caught up in his nothingness, is held there in the trap of the only progressive time, in the final analysis —that of the clock—against which he struggled so much because he felt all the horror of it. By the same token, the existent having surged forth from nothing, consciousness is detached from the vital genesis; "being" becomes the illusion of a prenatal distance; its pursuit, the alibi of a failure. The Baudelaire re-created by Sartre is in quest of no truly divine reality in man or in the universe; his "divine" is only a certain state of childhood, anterior to the separation which cast him into personal existence: a state of union almost undifferentiated from the idol-mother, he being her *"son by divine right."*

Baudelaire's movement is in fact much more complex as regards the psychic and the spiritual. In place of looking in his life at the symbolic intrication of the relations between beings, events, or states, like a travesty of his prelogical "choice," one can see there a *language* setting into action, on several levels, different realities bound up one with another. Every relation is presented then as a sum of *figures,* each capable of belonging to several relations and of fulfilling among these relations a mediative function. Persisting all Baudelaire's life, and constantly modified in it and by it, the relations of the poet with his childhood universe constitute the elementary syntax of his mind. They have their source in a fundamental principle which binds him to the real in perpetual genesis, in a *fatality* which separates him from it—the *fatal principle* by which he bceomes conscious both of his isolation and of this mysterious source. Read in *his* language, Baudelaire ceases to be a psychoanalytical or philosophical *case;* he is bound up with guilt and neurosis doubtlessly, but they *re-bind* him; in the bonds against which he struggles, he is a living symbol of the man in prey of the being—not of "being" according to Sartre, but of a "That" which, in the space of a cry, becomes a "Thou."[1]

When Sartre writes in the opening of his indictment: "And suppose he had deserved his life? Suppose, contrary to fixed ideas, men never had anything except the lives they deserve?," his interrogation is purely formal. He affirms man, self-creator, from the very moment of his origin, since in being born man surges forth, un-created. It is true that his demonstration on Baudelaire begins only at the death of the poet's father. Why not prior to birth, so that the primordial conditions of life might be themselves *deserved* since they are *chosen?* In Baudelaire, this could be a Gnostic intuition; but for Sartre, birth is an accident. We are *cast here,* until consciousness begins to distinguish and to choose; to liberate oneself is to annihilate the contingent of the childhood situation. It remains to be seen if, no matter what Sartre thinks, this annihilation is possible, or if, as Benjamin Fondane believes, "we are the seat of an infantile thought which we shall never allow to become adult and of an adult thought which will never have known an infantile stage." If it is thus— and so it is—the poetic task is not absurd; instead of sacrificing the integral being to the formation of reasoning man, it subjects the latter to the former *by the mystery of the child within us.* In this sense death, the hope of reintegration, appears like the end of a road at the juncture of this omnipresent and forbidden childhood: the living being can choose to engage itself—or, which is synonymous, can be chosen, engaged—in this quest whose goal is symbolized by the child. From that point it must be said, in a completely different sense from Sartre, that this living creature *deserves* all the obstacles in his path, which signifies that they are given to him; and that the progress of the quest is measured by their increase, by the growing sensation of distance, separation, absence, and fall. It is not the adult in us but the child that experiences limits, that is to say, of the adult age. The consciousness that he takes of it fortifies them unceasingly—until they break from their excess and until the division of the being ceases.

In Baudelaire, the quest of childhood is transversed by a contradictory movement of refusal. The fact of being born is charged with a fatality as intolerable as it is inflexible: "Who could without shuddering . . . look squarely at the hour of his birth?" wrote Thomas De Quincey, his spiritual brother. The coming of forms into the world is in opposition to the state of unity, a *fall;* it is an original death, Baudelaire even calls it a damnation. "In short, I believe that my life was damned right from the beginning, and that it is so forever" (letter to his mother, December 4, 1854). Existence on earth—not excluding every other form of possible existence in a series of incarnations—is a proof of the damnation inflicted on the poet. For poetic fatality is also an election: it is "after a decree of supreme powers" that the poet appears. He is one of these "divine souls," of whom "a superlative quality" is like "the term of their damnation" (*H.E.,* VII–VIII). They are "consecrated to the altar, condemned to advance toward death and glory across their own ruins" (*ibidem*). Who has them at his disposal in this manner, even from before the moment of their first sigh? It may be a "diabolical Providence," or the God "full of reasons and causes" who alone knows why every being exists, or Nature of whom one would say that she "makes life very hard for those from whom she wishes to extract great things" (*Œ.P.,* I, p. 268 on Poe). To borrow an image from De Quincey, three sisters, "goddesses of sorrow," aid Levana, goddess of childbirth, in her task: these are *Mater Lachrymarum, Mater Suspiriorum, Mater Tenebrarum* (*P.A.,* 182–185), the Fates. The reason (moral or cosmic) of the fall is the fall itself having become sentient, at least for the living creature and the time that he lives; or as Pierre Jean Jouve says in a striking, abbreviated form: the meaning of sin is "in the function of living," which is the test of tears, wails, and shadows. When Baudelaire speaks of original sin, he seems to understand not a transgression, a *human* revolt, but the principial identity between desire and life: therefore, the state of man because of his birth, expulsion out of another inconceivable state, anterior to the *conception.*

It would be tempting to suggest that the physical sign of this expulsion, the accouchement which drives the child from the mother, was the first and decisive sensation of the abyss experienced by Baudelaire, and generally by anyone born. It is not impossible that the trace of this impression persists in us during our entire lives, even in our attitudes and thoughts reputed to be the most adult. Perhaps even certain systems have for origin and for end, in authors, this tearing away from the being, a breaking away felt to be definitive well before being recognized and willed such. In Baudelaire this breaking away had as an effect an ambivalence which he became conscious of quite early. "Even as a child, I felt in my heart two contradictory sentiments, the horror of life and the ecstasy of life. It is truly the act of a hypersensitive sluggard" (*J.I.,* 96). Let us take note of these last two words: "sluggard" through unconscious nostalgia for a reality without substance or form, "hypersensitive" by vital reaction, electricity of the imagination, "which hovers over the highly-strung man and drives him to evil" (*H.E.,* xxix). This contradiction imbues solitude with life: "In spite of the family—and in the midst of friends, especially—a feeling of an eternally solitary destiny. Yet, a very live taste for life and pleasure" (*J.I.*, 58). Solitude is another form of separation which makes an exile of the very life which Baudelaire enjoyed keenly, but "with bitterness." Thus death, a virtual image of the anterior state, is read in exaltation or happiness, like a refusal or a reminiscence.

It will be said that the childhood and the adolescence of the poet were neither sad nor truly solitary, and that he depicted them in this fashion only in retrospect, in order to project into them and to legitimize his failure and his melancholy. That is to forget that the child or the adolescent does not perceive all the influences to which he is submitted, and that the adult, who undergoes the retardation of them, can, on the contrary, retrace their genesis, to the point of understanding in a single act of thought the different phases of his destiny. Such was indeed the plan of Baudelaire, which he desired all the more to realize since the contradiction troubled his existence at its source. Childhood innocence, his chimera, is not for him the absence of sin, but passion in its primitive strength, without "consciousness in evil." This "innocence" is a kind of madness: the child is a monster, a judgment that Baudelaire reports to us about Delacroix on himself as a child; only punishment and reason—but is not reason itself a punishment?—attenuate his "natural wickedness." And Baudelaire concludes: "Thus, by simple common sense, he [Delacroix] made a return toward the Catholic idea. For one can say that the child, in general, is, relative to man, in general, much closer to original sin" (*A.R.*, 37). I would not swear that this last sentence would come from a Catholic mind, but the judgment on childhood carries an Augustinian ring. In the child, concupiscence knows no restraint, and this avidity right from the first day is precisely sin itself, inseparable from the division. "Wicked avidity," said Saint Augustine; and this perpetuates itself, by generation, in nature itself, attained through man. For Baudelaire, as we already sense, it is Nature which is the fall, where man is carried away (even though Baudelaire's notion of nature, like all the fundamental concepts of the poet, is ambivalent). Generation perpetuates the fall: birth is an original sin, while at the same time a simple link in a chain. "Crime, the taste of which the human animal drew from its mother's womb, is originally natural" (*A.R.*, 96).

What are we to understand by "human animal"? That the proximity of original sin is animality, nature? Would "consciousness in evil" be the true germination of the mind in man, and this spiritualization a separation from another order than birth, a detachment? Yet Baudelaire, in the *Morale du joujou,* brings out "the spirituality of childhood," which he opposes to the reflexive ponderousness "of degenerated men." The mind exists then in the child, but in the undivided state, its faculties all in one, in which are mingled in a sudden illumination "desire, deliberation, and action." Close to original sin, childhood is likewise near the unitary mind, close to the secret essence of things. Jean-Pierre Richard is not wrong in seeing in this closeness the treasure of a "childhood beyond childhood," forbidden by original damnation. But for this same critic, the beyond and the Baudelairian interdict are only a décor and theatrical artifice, on a stage where the poet forbids himself and tempts himself as the spokesman of an indispensable Satan. This is an inadmissable thesis, unless to reduce to the pretext of an aesthetic delight the acute suffering of an entire life, the incapacity, more and more cruelly felt, of gathering up or reintegrating a lost substance. Baudelaire says twice, almost in the same terms, that "genius is only the willful recapture of childhood, childhood endowed now, to express itself, with virile organs and an analytic mind which permits it to bring order to the totality of materials involuntarily amassed" (*A.R.*, 60). In the *Paradis Artificiels,* "childhood regained at will" becomes "childhood clearly formulated": art is a superior state of childhood, an illumination of the unconscious treasure by the introduction of form, perhaps also by the *formula?* Genius would be then a sublimation of virility in the mind, a magician's wand, which would cause to appear at will this *new* which is the *real* domain of childhood and is now only the *imaginary* for "degenerated" man. Whence the complicity of the artist and the devil, like that of the devil and the child, this *budding Satan?* Whence the so frequent and so pathetic cry of the poet to his mother, against irreversibility, impassibility: "I want in a single effort a complete rejuvenation" (letter of December 20, 1855)?

On the Baudelairian stage, a single, sempiternal drama is repeated; it is not the magical game of the genius transmuting treasures reinvented from childhood, but a conflict of a fatal nature, the origin of which is lost for the one *who struggles and plays it.* It could be called the drama of the forbidden return to the womb or, alternately, of the return to the forbidden womb. The secret of Baudelaire's existence, *the initial orientation of his relation to God,* seems to me to be contained in his relation with his mother.

At the birth of the poet, his mother was twenty-eight years old, his father sixty-two; the father was to die in the poet's sixth year. Joseph-François Baudelaire, former seminarian of the diocese of Chalons, was, according to Marcel Ruff, elected constitutional curate of the vicarage of Dommartin-sous-Hans[2]; he had married for the first time in 1797, well before the Concordat. "I, son of a priest . . . ," Baudelaire will say defiantly. The statement, if true, must have marked his complex and sensitive nature, and modified his relations with his mother like his obscure reactions toward God. Baudelaire rarely alludes to his father, whom he includes, however, among his "intercessors" once in his prayer; for lack of documents, it is impossible to induce anything concerning their relations or concerning the influence of the father. One can imagine that the death of the father deprived the orphan of a mediator who would have aided him in establishing an intimate and personal relationship with God, and that the discovery of his abandonment of the priesthood did not simplify this relationship or even mark it with a sign. Must we see a bizarre, unconscious mimesis in Baudelaire's clerical appearance, that the most diverse observers take note of: Théophile Gautier, Nadar, Camille Lemonnier, Catulle Mendès, ten others in addition—an appearance which contrasted with the liking he had of shocking by "the most horrible blasphemies on the most naturally respectable things" (communication of Jules Toubat to Eugène Crépet)? The quasi-ritual satanism of Baudelaire in his art could be explained by this inverse priesthood more readily than by the fashion of the epoch. Did the death of the father provoke the "tendency toward mysticism" which was translated in Baudelaire the child by "conversations with God" (*J.I.*, 101)? What is certain is that this death made of Charles the sole mystical possessor of his mother: "Ah! that was for me the good time of maternal affections. I ask your pardon for calling *good time* that which was doubtlessly bad for you." These two sentences, standing in such contrast, from the famous letter of May 6, 1861, indicate as clearly as possible—for the letter constitutes a complete admission—that the child rejoiced over the death of the father, and allow one to believe that, guilty because of this joy, he could *make himself guilty* for this death.

"I was always alive in you; you were uniquely mine." Such is the state of union between the child and his widowed mother. The memory of this rapture will subsist like a cord never cut; it is literally that we must understand the forty-year-old poet speaking to his mother: "You, the sole being on whom my life hangs." The return of the child to the maternal bosom is the envelopment in the odor of the *mundus muliebris,* "in the soft atmosphere of woman," an androgynous disposition which, according to Baudelaire, favors the accomplishment of art. More precisely, it is "the imprint" of the feminine that the child passionately seeks in the intimate world "of his mother, of his maid, of his older sister"[3] (letter to Poulet-Malassis, April 23, 1860). Baudelaire the child takes pleasure in his mother's toilette like the lover in his mistress's; his mother's boudoir is the sanctuary of a mystical adoration. According to scattered bits of evidence in the work, the poet's sensuality passes easily from the erotic to the mystical, when it does not confuse the two. For example, "the femineity of the Church" is given "as the reason for its omnipotence," just before a remark on the color violet, "love contained, mysterious, veiled, canoness colored" (*J.I.,* 9), which evokes this other notation concerning a church in the Jesuit style, "a mystical, terrible boudoir." Inversely, the maternal boudoir, no less mystical and terrible, is a temple in which the mother is the divinity. This cult Baudelaire will perpetuate through an inverted fidelity to his mother by transferring it to the feminine type that he sought. Thus Cramer contemplates the nude Fanfarlo "in the depths of this delightful hovel which partook of the nature of the bad place and the sanctuary" (*P.A.,* 273): an ambiguity complacently nurtured which, departing from an infantile ecstasy, will finally become the essential element of the Baudelairian *counterreligion.*

The unitive life will not endure for long: after twenty months of widowhood, the poet's mother remarries—to the virtuous military officer, Aupick. Charles did not suffer from it, some will say.[4] But childhood nature is secretive, where suffering, all the while working on one, moves for a long time hidden. In such a case, strategy concerning a stepfather varies. Toward the one whom he calls "bosom friend," Baudelaire, no doubt unconsciously, chose affectionate submission as his tactic. That is to say, *repression,* a term that he uses quite some time before psychoanalysis, in reminding his mother of the necessity of "imposing upon himself constantly the repression of all expansiveness." Without a doubt he began his apprenticeship in it during childhood, but the alternation of the psychic collapse and of moral effort will be established only at the age of revolt against a guardianship which will dominate his mind forever. At twenty-four, he writes to his mother: "I have fallen into a fit of depression and a frightful dullness . . . it is impossible for me to make of myself what your husband would like for me to be" (letter to his mother, 1845). It is understood: to become his son. Consequently Baudelaire felt himself fallen from his right to his mother's love, a right usurped by the stepfather aided and abetted by the mother. Whence this mixture of guilt and hate, each nourishing the other, which ravages the eternal orphan? Unknown to Aupick, the meetings with his mother will be so many secret rendezvous, often not kept. Two months before the death of the general, Baudelaire wrote again: "I want to be the stronger!⁵ That is what I keep telling myself, but mechanically" (to his mother, February 8, 1857). His virility will not be restored: Aupick will carry it away, into the tomb. With Aupick dead, Baudelaire does not reassert his right; he proclaims that of his mother over him: "Believe that I am yours absolutely, and that I belong only to you" (to his mother, June 3, 1857).

The cord is not cut, but reunion is impossible. In the dream about the brothel, a composite dream and a mirror of destiny, admirably related to Asselineau in a letter of March 13, 1856, Baudelaire clearly identifies himself with "a monster born in the house, and who sits eternally on a pedestal. Although alive, it is a part of the museum."⁶ This living monster is also a creature "which has lived," a dead living thing, like the abortions that inhabit *Limbos* (the first title of *Les Fleurs du Mal*). "A monstrous appendage . . . comes out of its head, something elastic like rubber, and so long, so very long, that if he were to roll it around his head like a wisp of hair, it would be far too heavy, and absolutely impossible to carry; that, from then on, he is obliged to roll it around his limbs, which, moreover, creates a very beautiful appearance." According to Dr. Laforgue's interpretation, this consubstantial appendage is Jeanne Duval. Alternatively, given the ambivalence of symbols, I see in this the cord that attaches Baudelaire to his mother, of whom Jeanne Duval is the antonym. The cord may signify the refusal to be born into an independent existence and the nostalgia for an existence already lived. Black, it is gangrenous and no longer brings nourishment but suffocation. This is an ambivalence which will be found again in the dialectic of guilt and resentment: existence is lived double in part—simultaneously in submission and in revolt.

Laforgue and Sartre have emphasized that Baudelaire chose to live under a guardianship—or must we say that his symbolic constellation disposed him to do so? The legal guardian is the definitive instrument of this subordination which was to last throughout the poet's life, keeping him in the limbo of the life already lived. He himself confesses (but where is the antiphrasis here?): *"I should not like for my legal guardian to be taken away* nor all my debts to be paid *at once. Beatitude would create idleness"* (to his mother, May 8, 1861). Two days earlier, he was asking his mother to become *his true legal guardian.* An attempt —condemned by nature to failure—to remake the unity by legal means: we see in it one of the mechanisms of Baudelaire's ethics. The law itself gives rise to the prohibition; and when Baudelaire recalls thus the legal guardian to his mother: "this dreadful mistake which has ruined my life, sullied all my days and given the color of hate and despair to all my thoughts," he evokes certainly an original damnation, but of which the fault belongs to the one who damns as much as to the one damned. What is, moreover, the nature of this damnation? The young man cannot dispose freely of the paternal heritage; that is to say, of the father's power: he is frustrated, doubly orphan, cut off from the womb and the inheritance; castrated in short, both in his resemblance to the father and in his desire for the mother; therefore amputated from this *genius* which is "childhood regained at

will," endowed "with virile and powerful organs." From this
instant, in the light of Baudelaire's destiny, the atrocious apostrophe that the mother hurls against God in *Bénédiction* begins
to become clear:

> Since of all women You have chosen me
> To be repugnant to my sorry spouse,
> And since I cannot cast this misshapen monster
> Into the flames, like an old love letter,
>
> I shall spew the hatred with which you crush me down
> On the cursed instrument of your malevolence,
> And twist so hard this wretched tree
> That it cannot put forth its pestilential buds!

This "misshapen monster" is the mutilated child, deprived of
the power of appeasing the boundless passion that Baudelaire
confesses for his mother. In the situation created by the remar-
riage, he is ashamed both for his mother's feelings and his own.
The mother prostitutes herself to Aupick in the eyes of the
legitimate master, the child exiled from her although heir to the
paternal right.

> I think of my great swan with his crazy motions,
> Ridiculous, sublime, like a man in exile,
> Relentlessly gnawed by longing! and then of you,
>
> Andromache, base chattel, fallen from the embrace
> Of a mighty husband into the hands of proud Pyrrhus,
> Standing bowed in rapture before an empty tomb,
> Widow of Hector, alas! and wife of Helenus!
>
> [*Le Cygne.*]

The power of this collective singular noun *base chattel* says a
great deal about the downfall of the mother in the eyes of the

son, who can endure this abasement only by taking it upon himself through shame, by degrading himself on the sexual plane. From this comes no doubt his inability to love completely any other woman: like his existence, his being is contradictory, flesh and spirit reciprocally exiled. He prostitutes himself to Jeanne Duval the way he sees his mother prostituted to Aupick: symbolic identity, but at the same time an irreparable separation from the idol mother, *Virgo Mater*. Sorrowfully, irresistibly, a certain farewell addressed to the mother as to "the only person whom I love"[8] (letter of August 8, 1864) evokes this cry in *De profundis clamavi:*

> I beg pity of Thee, the only one I love,
> From the depths of the dark pit where my heart has fallen.

Who is this only one here? Jeanne Duval or the mother? or both? The structure of *Les Fleurs du Mal* not being arbitrary, it is significant that this poem follows immediately *Une Charogne,* in which the putrid flesh bears witness, in its own fashion, to a "divine essence," a loving, imperishable form that the poet has preserved. It is because in prostituting himself to Jeanne, the poet —by this very fact—renders to the mother a cult of latria.

The image of the abyss—here of a life absent from itself, interminably in the process of falling, indistinct from the monotonous unwinding of time—corresponds to the metaphysical ennui of being born, a belated fruit of the separation from the mother: of being born and not completely born—caught between the fright before his temporal damnation and the horror of a womb which would change into a tomb. Indeed, Baudelaire attributes to his mother the power to save him from a solitude where the father—*that is to say God himself*—is silent: "I need to be saved, and you alone can save me. I want to say everything today. I am alone, without friends, without a mistress, without a dog or a cat: who will have pity on me? I have only my father's portrait, which is always silent" (to his mother, May 6, 1861). But he knows also that his mother desires only to see him *"like everybody else"* (to his mother, November 4, 1856), thus the opposite of unique, singular. At the very moment when he opens himself up to her entirely, he tells her that she has never appreciated or known him. That is why his fine plans for life together, indefinitely postponed, will materialize into a few weeks only. If he is bound up forever, it is not with the real mother, whom he will summon, in an outburst of pathetic anger, to become once again *"immediately, and completely, a mother"* (to his mother, January 9, 1851), but he is bound to the *Géante* of his childhood, idol of eternal youth and death. Thus, in *Laquelle est la vraie?* the lover of Bénédicta "remains attached, forever perhaps, to the grave of the ideal."

In the symbolism of the feminine body in Baudelaire's work, one will notice the role of the knees. The knees are the porch of a secret, of "a gulf we may not sound," tied no doubt to the poet's past in the same manner as to his "end of autumn," but which transcends them—one on this side of birth, the other beyond death. "Nestled" against their knees, buried in their skirts, breathing the odor of female among certain women who evoke for him autumn—this season which is between life and death—Baudelaire seeks to return to the ideal mother, which to him is lap and tomb. Let us read *Le Balcon;* as much as to Jeanne, it seems consecrated to the mother, substratum of all that is feminine:

> Mother of memories, mistress of mistresses,
> O you, all my pleasure, O you, all my duty!

The memory of "the peace of the fireside" can be also the memory of the "good time," of childhood, the object of a constant effort at resurrection, of identification by the "genius":

I know the art of evoking happy moments,
And live again our past, my head laid on your knees.

The same in *Chant d'automne:*

Yet, love me, tender heart! be a mother,
Even to an ingrate, even to a scapegrace;

is perhaps, through Marie Daubrun, dedicated in fact to the mother on whose knees Baudelaire is filled with agony and enchantment on the threshold of death. "The tomb awaits; it is avid!" And the coffin nailed shut with such haste, *for whom?* Is it for the mother and the son joined in the impossible embrace? "We are evidently destined to love each other, to live one for the other, to end our lives in the most honorable and the gentlest way possible. And yet, in the terrible circumstances in which I am placed, I am convinced that one of the two of us will kill the other, and that finally we will kill each other, reciprocally" (to his mother, May 6, 1861).

This death reciprocally inflicted, sacrificial, would seemingly be only the final rite of a long liturgy of griefs and sorrows. Suffering through his mother and making her suffer filled Baudelaire's life; and these are the saving figures, the substitutions of maternal love, that his imagination takes pleasure in running through with the blade for lack of being able to penetrate their forbidden femininity. It is through the wound that he reopens the barred access to his former life, and one could see in it a symbolic act vengeful of the mutilation that he has undergone but, likewise, a desperate aggression *against the origin* itself. The treatment inflicted on "Celle qui est trop gaie," on the Angel of *Réversibilité* "to the emanations" of whom Baudelaire asked for a return of youth, would merit a rigorous analysis. The "joyous flesh" and the "pardonned breast" that the poet chastizes in dream symbol-

ize the conjugal pleasure of the mother as well as the loves of
Madame Sabatier. To punish the mother is to reinfuse her with
the culpable "venom" which she has gotten rid of; it is to
reimpregnate her with the abortion that she has cursed. Thus, by
this return to the womb that represents death, the original stain
will be effaced. Or else, in *A une madone,* by a sacrilegious
parody of suffering that the Virgin of the Seven Sorrows undergoes beneath the eye of her Son:

> I, torturer full of remorse, shall make seven
> Well sharpened Daggers and, like a callous juggler,
> Taking your deepest love for a target,
> I shall plant them all in your panting Heart,
> In your sobbing Heart, in your bleeding Heart!

In Baudelaire's religious conception, the story of childhood
forms a magnetic field around which the major themes are
arranged. If direct faith in a personal God seems weakly felt, if
even, as we shall see, the idea of this God depends more on
speculation than experience, that can come from the imprecision
or the repression of the paternal memory, and all together, in a
closely related manner, to the child's passion for his mother, an
all-powerful, maternal image of the One. It is the maternity of
God, his cosmic, unifying impersonality, that Baudelaire has first
of all experienced; and in the same way, the unbearable dehis-
cence that is the fall of a creature expulsed by God. Whence the
dual aspect of original sin: by casting beings out from himself,
God himself falls in multiplicity. This process does not appear
the less fatal or, if one wishes, *natural.* The multiplicity would
seem to be only an expansion of cosmic immanence, were there
not consciousness, which is so alive in some beings who have
been broken away and engulfed. Baudelaire is one of these
beings, perhaps from the fact of having been twice expulsed

from his mother without having been really detached from her in the process. The existence in which he is *suspended* remains intermediary, an obscure parenthesis in the heart of the unity. Tied to this unity by a psychic bond which cannot be cut and which suffocates him in the limbo of a "real," anemic life, he does not participate less, because of this very bond which makes him here waste away, in the unitary existence by which he is both nourished and deprived. It is because of the excessive richness of universal analogy that he fails to constitute himself *here even* into an autonomous and limited personality; or rather, this original dependence is given to him so that he will experience the one by the other, the superabundance of being so and the wretchedness of being deprived of it. Thus he is going to make of his entire life an effort in two directions that are apparently contradictory: the return to the One and the painstaking analysis of exile. He will suffer, as if being drawn and quartered by it, in everything he does, but nowhere more than in his relations to woman. His erotic life and work justify Pierre Jean Jouve's assertion: "Baudelaire cannot religiously love the essence with with he is smitten, except by borrowing the ways which reveal the demoniacal."

2. Counterreligion

"What more widowed soul!" said Georges Blin with commiseration. In the poet's work, widows are maternal figures, protected by their solitary majesty (*Les Veuves, P.P.P.*). The Andromaque of *Le Cygne* is the mother-widow beloved by Baudelaire the child. Thirty years later—after the death of Aupick, the son is of the age that she keeps in memory, and it is her image that he meets in the streets, setting out like *Le Beau Navire,*

Tall, slender, in heavy mourning, majestic grief,
A woman passed, with a glittering hand
Raising, swinging the hem and flounces of her skirt.
(*A une passante.*)

She appears again, in *Les Petites Vieilles,* an old mother-widow,
watched over tenderly by her son:

My anxious eyes are fixed on your uncertain steps,
As if I were your own father; how wonderful!

this father with whom the poet identifies in order to imagine
more readily the "novice passions" of the mother-fiancée. The last
line of *A une passante:* "O you whom I would have loved, O you
who knew it!," while being addressed to any woman who might
awaken for a moment the ideal dream of the mother could really
embody the entire past of the mother in this intemporal nostalgia,
an eternal jealousy. Baudelaire is the eternal widower-lover of a
mother to whom his cult goes, for whom other women are
the substituted idols.

"Precocious interest in women. I used to confuse the odor of
fur with the odor of woman. I remember. . . . In short, I loved
my mother for her elegance. So I was a precocious dandy." What
an eloquent suspension of thought, after "I remember" (*J.I.,* 27)!
The perfume, "spiritual flesh" of the mother, permits the child
who clothes himself in it to realize the double phantasm of
physical possession and the return to the womb. But the memory
remains in suspension: the act is unsuccessful, the attention
diverted on the external appearance of the mother, whose elegance contains—in the Baudelairian sense—an idea of "spirituality." To complete the reversal of attitude, the "precocious dandy"
contradicts in the end the "precocious interest in women" pro-

fessed in the beginning. Because "woman is natural, that is to say abominable. Therefore she is always vulgar; that is, the opposite of the dandy" (*J.I.,* 53).

At the highest point of erotic evocation, Baudelaire refuses the natural. What can be said? Without a doubt the image of the mother given over to pleasure, and also to procreation. The ambivalence of the sentiment is here extreme. Let us set one against the other, "the vast majesty of your widow's grieving" and "the frigid majesty of the sterile woman," the virgin-mother of the repressed desire and the "barren virgin" that the poet substitutes for her. To abolish the retrospective jealousy, not only does Baudelaire "forget" the embraces of Aupick, he also denies himself in a way; the mother, in her widowhood, is thus rendered virgin. Her son can then love her forever without becoming a "disgusting Phoenix, son and father of himself." Inversely, so as not to become a mother, the idol of pleasures must be infertile, sterilized. Frigid even, to symbolize the maternal interdict. In both cases, the essential is incommunicable. The genital localization is "a malice or a satire of Providence against love" and "the manner of generation a sign of original sin" (*J.I.,* 71). To divert this malice—must we understand: this aptitude of the "demoniacal Providence" to do evil?—is the duty of the dandy, who remains alone but who, we shall see, prostitutes himself, without breaking down his solitude.

This is an extreme androcentric concept: Baudelaire, for some reason, saw himself forbidden or forbad himself to do his apprenticeship with woman through his mother. But in relations with women, the mother remains an intermediary; whence the contradictory nature of these relations. As long as he is a virgin, love is sacred; when he forces the interdict, it becomes a crime. The insistence with which Baudelaire represents the act of sexual intercourse as "a torture or a surgical operation," a "question applied by painstaking torturers," the rape of one of the partners by the other, shows both his inability to break through the forbidden and also the relentlessness with which he goes about trying to break through it. It is upon himself that he applies the forceps to extricate himself from the cult of the mother. But inversely, he punishes himself for this apostasy by self-mutilation or by undergoing such from his demons, like this sole inhabitant of Cythera with whom he identifies:

> On your isle, O Venus! I found upright only
> A symbolic gallows from which hung my image . . .
> [*Un Voyage à Cythère.*]

However, the cult of the mother and that of the woman form only one, sometimes turning to its own blasphemy. Death, the ideal expression of this cult, has for its unreal pole the impossible return to the womb and, for its real pole, the end of this "ecstasy of life" of which birth is the beginning: *ecstasy* by expulsion from the born creature, which, in the appeasement of desire, tries to open for itself a way, in a reverse fashion, back to its source. If woman, in Baudelaire's work, is not just the other sex, but the Other, absolutely, she is also—at least figuratively—primordial Unity whose way this Other blocks. The fact that the work can appear above all like the expression of an erotic cult must not make one forget—far from it!—the irrepressible, prohibited passion of which the eroticism is the mask and the dead end. To say like Sartre that Baudelaire displays more sensuality than moderation is to fail to recognize that in the case in point "moderation" is submitted to prohibition. Doubtless this prohibition, whose psychic roots remain hidden, takes on, in the poet's imagination, the ritual forms that the work reproduces. The cult has its internal logic, that of archaic symbols, reanimated in it. This symbolic consciousness almost completely immersed in the unconscious explains in what way, in his work and in his life,

Baudelaire seems to illustrate Joseph de Maistre: strangly, by the erotic ritual, in which the poet plays, sometimes on the other and sometimes on himself, the role of sacrificer. Maistre emphasized the verbal identity, in Hebrew, of sin and sacrifice for the sin, sacrifice in which one always finds *"a grievous and bloody operation, carried out on the reproductive organs.* That is: *Anathema on human generations,* and SALVATION BY BLOOD" (*Soirées,* II, 9).

All commentators have noted what Charles du Bos calls "the severe disjunction of the orders" of the flesh and the spirit. Perhaps it is less a question of disjunction than of "dialectical agony," according to the very felicitous expression of Georges Blin. A dialectic frequently made clear in the *Journaux intimes:* "We love women in proportion to their being unknown and distant to us. It is a pederastic pleasure to love intelligent women. Thus, bestiality excludes pederasty" (*J.I.,* 13). Since "the woman in whom we do not find pleasure is the one we love" (*Œ.P.,* III, 15), to debauch oneself with others, to destroy her, is to adore her all the more. But woman can also be unknown and distant through her flesh; the mind can love the horror that it experiences from it. (*To find pleasure, to love,* are here used in a dual sense: mind and body have as object not even pleasure—nor even suffering—in the same creature which procures them.) This dialectical use of the *even* and the *same* is common to the homosexual and to the dandy. Bestiality it is that brings the mind out of itself, sends it into ecstasies; since woman is the opposite of the dandy, to debauch oneself with her, to destroy oneself, is to adore oneself all the more mentally.

Woman is therefore heterogeneous in every respect; Baudelaire adulates her and at the same time scorns her. *He uses her,* as he confesses to Madame Sabatier. Woman is the image that the poet makes of her, angel or beast according to the needs of his "consciousness." As for the feminine being in her natural state, "woman is hungry and she wants to eat, thirsty and she wants to drink. She is in heat and wants to be fucked. A fine thing!" She is, then, only *living matter*, endowed with desire and with attraction. But this matter is enigmatic: by multiplying concupiscence, she augments the nostalgia for unity. The mind which becomes completely lost in it finds itself likewise: if it contemplates her without becoming lost, it causes to emanate from her its own depths.

Because this matter is a world, the *mundus muliebris*, which contains and modifies the other. This erotic world is the matrix of Baudelaire's spiritual universe. Their interaction produces a complex symbolism, contradictory, a mirror with a dual attitude toward sex and toward life. If Baudelaire's spirituality is poetic more than religious, it is because it has not freed itself from this matricial environment and from its primordial eroticism. Like the poet, it is not completely born. More than mystical and spiritual, Baudelaire's consciousness is magic and psychic: it is "consciousness in evil," it needs chaos in order to be, and its dialectic is an alchemy. "The saddest of alchemists" exercises his powers over the matter from which he draws them, woman or nature, woman-nature; and if he can "change gold to iron and make of paradise a hell," the reverse is no less true. The bottom and the top both call and pursue each other: a perpetual movement of this "religion" is a closed vessel. To the famous lines:

I adore you as much as the nocturnal vault,
O vase of sadness, most taciturn one,

let us compare, in *Curiosités Esthétiques,* the allusion (with respect to Tassaert) to the charm that comes from licentious engravings and the melancholy feeling that results: "The sight of these pictures starts me down the slopes of immense revery, almost like an obscene book casts us out upon mystical, blue oceans" (*C.E.,* 123–124). On a plane elevated in a way different from that of Ingres, Baudelaire's "libertinage" "is serious and full of conviction" (*C.E.,* 213). From that comes the poet's keen judgment of the eighteenth-century libertines, and especially Laclos.[9] He recognizes in them, masked or otherwise, the rigorous logic of an eroticism which, out of hatred for nature, pushes the natural to an excess; a movement which, in him, reaches the extreme of bestiality only to bring him toward another extreme, an angelic one. And if he follows the advice of La Mettrie, who in his *L'Art de jouir,* invites man to make "[his] soul, if he can, as slimy and lascivious as [his] body," this return to the womb by amnion and sperm is a kind of labor against the grain which fills the spirit with ecstasy in its upward flight.

With the exception of his mother and Mariette, "the kindhearted servant" who perhaps has a role in *Les Vocations* (*P.P.P.*), two types of women, or rather two *ideas* of women, haunt Baudelaire's life and mind. The first, projections of celestial glory, like Marie Daubrun and Madame Sabatier; the second, projections of infernal glory, Sara la Louchette and, especially, Jeanne Duval. This latter is, with his mother and against her, the only woman whom he loved constantly, inside the myth that he made of her, which derives, by analogy and unconscious opposition, from the immense maternal symbolism. The relation between *Delphine* and *Hippolyte* illustrates in its true spiritual perspective the "infernal" relation between Jeanne and him. The name of Hippolyte, the "prisoner," suggests even a rapprochement with the legend of this saint in the *Légende dorée,* in which the woman-demon is changed into a rotting carcass before the eyes of the man she has just seduced: vampiric seduction and corollary transmutation that *Les Métamorphoses du vampire* translates with a macabre realism worthy of a medieval imagist. The double vampirism of *Madrigal Triste* and *L'Héautontimorouménos* is the sado-masochistic aspect of the "demoniacal" possession enclosing the two lovers, but more closely Baudelaire who, it seems, tears away only in order to liberate himself from a frightful feeling of constriction. The "dreaded" arms of the woman, even described in a pleasant manner in which the anxiety is apparent,

> Are the worthy rivals of glistening boas,
>   Made to clasp stubbornly
> Your lover, as if to imprint him on your heart.
> (*Le Beau Navire*.)

We shall find again this sensation of progressive suffocation linked sometimes with the idea of the prison cell, of the sepulchre, of the none-life, sometimes with the image of the abyss and the endless descent. The metamorphosis of the vampire is only one of the transmutations of "the alchemy of suffering" dear to the poet, alchemy of which man is the "subtle spirit," woman the apparatus which distills it. It is she who, in the *Danse macabre*, reduced to her skeleton's armor, appears identical to Death. And the

> Inexhaustible well of folly and of sins!
> Eternal alembic of ancient suffering!

is another form of the

> Blind, deaf machine, fecund in cruelties!
> Remedial instrument, drinker of the world's blood,
>   [*"Tu mettrais l'univers entier . . . ."*]

whose function is to sweep man along from fall to fall in order to purify him by the contrary ascension of suffering. This woman-machine empties man by devouring him, which can be interpreted as a symbolic return into the womb, to the "wine skin with gluey sides." Thus erotic "death," a caricature of the return to the womb, aggravates, by deluding it in the moment, the definitive despair of life. Woman "learned in pleasure," who believes herself learned in evil, because she knows the science "of losing old Conscience in the depths of a bed," does not abolish but increases in man this "consciousness of doing evil" that she knows nothing about.

Vampire, machine, woman is also qualified as a "strong little man, manikin"[10]: a word which comes from *manneken,* a diminutive of the Dutch for *man.* One thinks of Luther's *Männin;* of the Eve of Martínez de Pasqualís, according to whom God made Adam, who, wishing in his turn to give life to spiritual beings, succeeded in creating a dark form opposed to his own, whom he named Houva, "hommesse," or female man. Baudelaire doubtlessly was not unaware of this Martinist symbol, a variant of the eternal matter-spirit couple. Eve is not at the origin of evil in it, she is the product of it, to whose likeness man is changed in order to engender from her a posterity. A memorial of the transgression, woman serves to reiterate it in a carnal creation which is ever and ever more degraded. Although in one sense innocent, Eve is none the less born in the incitement of the evil spirits of which man had custody. Such a symbolic schema is found, or very nearly, in the demonological speculation anterior to the poet. Let us observe only that the Baudelairian woman, in one respect, is idealized into a demoniac instrument, truly a demon incarnate.

Why this inverted idealization? Because procreated nature, a consequence of the fall, is fatally the kingdom of evil. The work of the sex organs, procreation unrolls a chain without end in a pit without bottom. The one who deliberately palliates natural fatality by sterility—this is Baudelaire's case—becomes only more conscious of the spiritual fatality which sweeps him along. Or rather, this consciousness which is intensified is identical to this fatality. No matter what the psychic causes at the origin of his choice, Baudelaire has refused to be the "disgusting Phoenix, son and father of himself" cited earlier. He has, so far as possible, extracted himself from the acceleration of the innumerable. To pay the price of this solitude, he must and wishes to assume consciousness in doing evil, submerged as that consciousness is in the great multiplicity by the blind process of generations. Instead of being just any one of successive individuals who are begotten then annihilated in time, he is the unique spirit through them, denied the grave (cf. *Un Voyage à Cythère*), and who falls throughout eternity. Precipitated, the spirit becomes demoniacal. We shall see what spiritual idea Baudelaire has of the fall, which could be that of the One in multiplicity, a fall causing and encompassing that of beings in formal existence and reproduction. Whatever may be the case, the indivisible fascinating entity of the act of falling is the abyss; and woman, one of its representations, homogeneous with its nothingness like matter, with its grandeur like spirit. Whence two contrasting entries in *Mon Coeur mis à nu,* the first: "Woman does not know how to separate the soul from the body. She is simplistic, as animals are. A satirist would say that it is because she has only the body" (*J.I.,* 82). And the second: "The eternal Venus (caprice, hysteria, fantasy) is one of the seductive forms of the devil" (*ibid.*). It is true that, without a soul, "living matter" is demoniacal; the poet, in *L'Examen de Minuit,* remembers having

> Kissed with great devotion
> Stupid and unfeeling Matter.

In so many words, kissed the devil's rear end. The devil seizes *empty matter,* the hysterical psyche; formless, he gives it infinitely variable form in bestiality: "Do satans not have the form of animals? Cazotte's camel—camel, devil and woman" (*J.I.,* 25).

There was a time when "the eternal Venus" was still the celestial Aphrodite: "I love to think of those naked epochs," said

Baudelaire upon beginning the evocation of this golden age that he identifies with the reign of Pan, that is to say, of *"one* energy," of absolute immanence. The poet in *L'Ecole païenne* ridiculed "these young men who can be called learned and intelligent" who await the return of the Great Pan, whose death, in the time of Augustus, the seas had announced. These adepts claimed "it is necessary to return to the true doctrines, which were obscured for *a moment* by the infamous Galilean" (*A.R.,* 290). Nearly ten years later, in his study on *Tannhaüser,* the poet claims as his own the idea of an irreparable cleavage in the history of the conscience: with Christ, Panic energy is repressed, Aphrodite becomes infernal. "The radiant antique Venus, Aphrodite born from the white foam, did not come through the horrific gloom of the Middle Ages with impunity. . . . By descending underground, Venus came close to hell, and she goes doubtlessly, on certain abominable, solemn occasions, to pay homage regularly to the Archdemon, the prince of flesh and the lord of sin" (*A.R.,* 215-216).

In rereading *J'aime le souvenir* . . . , let us note that the Pantheist epoch seen by Baudelaire is that of equilibrium, health, beauty; and that the world after the death of the Great Pan, if it is the world of the conscience, is also that of disequilibrium, illness, ugliness. The golden age described in this poem is no doubt only a conscious dream, a memory in the Baudelairian sense, a reintegration through *remembrance.* Here are not represented a *before* and an *after,* but a state of perfection, innocence, and a state of fall, sin. The coming of Christ did not mark the downfall, but precipitated the consciousness of the fall. Henceforth, "man and woman know from birth that in evil is found all pleasure" (*J.I.,* II). To talk like Dmitri Karamazov, no one escapes from the contradiction between the ideal of the Madonna and that of Sodom, a contradiction which is an enigma—perhaps even the unique enigma—of God. Baudelaire speaks of chaotic sensuality in terms which will later be those of Dostoevski, to whom on occasion he can be compared: this poet in prey to the paradox of two loves is not "an ordinary libertine, *flitting from one mistress to another,* but a general, universal man, living morganatically with the absolute Ideal of pleasure, with the Queen of all female devils, with all female fauns and with all female satyrs, who are relegated underground since the death of the Great Pan, that is, with the indestructible and irresistible Venus" (*A.R.,* 224).

That this relegation *underground,* in a part of the being and the world marked forbidden, therefore ambivalent in the *sacred* sense, corresponds to the personal conflict of the poet, does not alter the universally lived significance. By sacrilegious magic, Satan is master of the impossible reintegration, the tempter and guardian of the forbidden. And woman, in reality and figuratively, is the agent and the place of this impossible reintegration, coveted as much as feared. Whence the ambivalence of woman, a fountainhead of all antinomies under each of her contradictory appearances. Seen as demon, sometimes she engulfs irreparably the poet outside himself, sometimes she possesses him and incarcerates him in his own ego, of which she is the tomb. Abyss or sepulchre, she isolates him in a continual dream, in an enchanted existence of which the magic potion is a vertiginous lasciviousness, a powerful stimulant of guilt:

> Great angel who carries on your proud face
> The blackness of Hell from which you come
> Fierce and gentle tamer who placed me in a cage
> To serve as a spectacle for your cruelty,
> Nightmare of my nights, sirene with no bust,
> Who tugs me, always standing at my side,
> By my saintly robe or my sage's beard,
> To offer me the poison of a shameless love.
>
> (*Œ.P.,* I, 5.)

The poison is woman herself, whether she brings about the loss of "the ancient conscience," "powerful oblivion," sleep; whether she exasperates in the poet's mind the struggle of concupiscence and disgust, of which she is the common source. As poison, she saturates the whole being: she impregnates the atmosphere and divides the blood. She is thus, through an apparent contradiction, the matter to which the mind clings and the spiritual essence which *possesses* it: the feminine body conceals an eternal form, a veritable succubus bound to the being to whom it is attached, through death. Such is, it seems, the meaning of the last stanzas of *Une Charogne,* of the two tercets of *Je te donne ces vers* . . . , of the sonnet *Le Possédé,* and more generally of numerous poems symbolizing the narrow reciprocal dependence of the mistress and of the lover, a dependence which is more than a "companion-ship in the transgression" (Charles du Bos)—a perverse emula-tion, a common curse where the roles are shared. It is indeed a question there of a love, in crescendo admirably analyzed in the pages on Tannhaüser, and whose "ineluctable satanic logic" re-sults from its exacerbated ambivalence:

> Beloved poison prepared by the angels! Liqueur
> That consumes me, O the life and death of my heart!
> > (*Le Flacon.*)

Life which causes death, death which makes live: the amorous embrace (*Duellum*) gives the illusion of death only to precipitate the soul toward new abysses, in order to make reciprocal hate eternal, a demoniacal form of shared expiation.

One could explain this fatal interdependence by Baudelaire's inability to extricate himself from Jeanne Duval. (See the dream cited above.) But when he says of Jeanne, as early as 1848, that "for a long time" he has loved her "only out of a sense of duty"[11] and that in this liaison "expiation and the desire to remunerate her devotion play the great role" (letter to Aupick, December 8, 1848), this announces already the expiatory destiny that his imagination symbolizes, beginning with the dark, shadowy depths. To understand to what extent it is a double destiny, it is necessary to read in a parallel manner *L'Héautontimorouménos* and *Madrigal Triste*, two poems in which the cruel love is displayed in its irremissible ferocity. two scenes of spiritual vampirism which relate directly to *Le Vampire*, to the woman dressed for the sabbath, "strong as a herd of demons," whom Baudelaire qualifies as

> Infamous bitch to whom I'm bound
> Like the convict to his chain.

But here, the vampire is the poet, seized by "the voracious Irony" in which he is permitted to see Jeanne Duval in furious scenes, doubtlessly exciting,

> She's in my voice, the termagant!
> All my blood is her black poison!
> I am the sinister mirror
> In which the vixen looks.

and behind her this demon to whom he shouts with all his might, like Alvare to the amorous Devil disguised as Biondetta: *"Dear Beelzebub, I adore you!"* The *Héautontimorouménos* is eternally devouring himself, his poison is his own blood. Blood: the Maistrian *réité,* guilt inherent in the human being. Thus the everlasting part of man, concupiscence which forever engulfs him, is linked to woman to the point of being merged with her; but the destiny is mutual, man is a demon for woman. If "the crown of perversity belongs to woman," man is superior to her in atrocities because of the consciousness in evil. *Madrigal Triste,* like *A celle qui est trop gaie,* distills this venom of consciousness in the guise of reciprocity: it is "the irresistible disgust," analogous to "the irresistible Night," that the poet would like to instill in his *beloved.* From this, one comes to the point of thinking that this frightful couple realizes in damnation "a kind of androgyneity" which would be the caricature of its paradisiacal archetype vaguely dreamed by Baudelaire to exist in the perfume of the *mundus muliebris.*

Of all the ambivalent symbols in the Baudelairian erotic world (the moon, the serpent, among others), the most powerful is odor. It envelops, impregnates, intoxicates; it is the substratum of demonic "spirituality," flesh saturated and diffuse, false psychic *aura* emanating from the female body. This quasi-spiritual essence is only an extension, to the point of being ubiquitous, of insidious animal seduction, in that the symbol of perfume is analogous to that of the cat. Let us cite as proof of it only this fragment of the prose poem, *L'Horloge:*

> For me, if I bend down to the beautiful Feline, so appropriately named, who is at once the honor of her sex, the pride of my heart and the perfume of my mind, whether it be by night, or by day, in full light or in opaque shadows, deep in her adorable eyes, I always see the hour distinctly, always the same, a vast, solemn hour, large as space, without division into minutes and seconds—an immobile hour which is not marked on clocks, and yet light as a breath, rapid as a glance.

Odor, infinity emanated from the mother, then from the woman, encloses the lover in an omnipresent totality, an eternal simultaneity.

> Profound, magical charm, with which the past,
> Restored to life, makes us inebriate!
> Thus the lover from an adored body
> Plucks memory's exquisite flower.
>   (*Le Parfum, Un fantôme.*)

Since perfume is a subtle substance, it serves as a particularly efficacious stimulant to memory, through space and time, being linked to the system of correspondences and especially this mystical experience of memory whose access the correspondences open. We shall see further on how this counterreligion conceals the abyss and deepens it: the past present annihilates the real present. Let us be content here to point out the maleficent nature of odors, the instrument of Satan's visitations. Nowhere better than in *La Destruction* can we grasp the intent and role of the perfume that "floats" or that "prowls," entity become spirit:

> The Demon is always moving about at my side;
> He floats about me like an impalpable air;
> I swallow him, I feel him burn my lungs
> And fill them with an eternal, sinful desire.

This sonnet first had for a title *La Volupté*, which refers us to the invocation addressed to the "Goddess who permeates the air" in *La Prière d'un Païen*:

> Ah! do not dampen your ardor;
> Warm my numb heart again,
> Pleasure, torture of souls!
> Goddess! hear me, I beseech you!

Goddess or demon, voluptuous odor stirs concupiscence endlessly—this vital flame, torturing but arousing the damned for whom the earth is a dungeon; a blissful punishment which liberates the heart from its lethargy, from its sepulchral claustrophobia. The "elastic phantom," emanating from woman or clothing her like a more subtle body, is sometimes associated with the sensual perfume of churches, divine boudoirs. It is also associated with the work of corruption which releases essence from matter: therefore, with death, over which it triumphs by bearing witness to it. One would be tempted to see in this intemporal-like entity an analogy with the *citta* in the Hindu *sankhya,* a subtle substance which would gather the memory and augment the *Karma,* the ignorance of covetousness, the "eternal, sinful desire" of *La Destruction.* It would be a question then of the very principle of this latter, a principle which survives the exterior that it seeks to destroy, espousing it in order to corrupt it better, such as the mind the matter in which it is incorporated: "There are strong perfumes for which all matter is porous . . ." (cf. *Le Flacon*). Taken in this total significance it is evident that the perfume transcends the fragrant essence of the perfumer, which serves it as a sensitive vehicle. It is an emanation of the being; its particles are spiritual. This can even be a living spirit, the occupant of the fleshly habitation, as in the sonnet full of ambiguities dedicated to *Le Chat* as much as to the mistress whom Baudelaire sees "in spirit" while caressing it:

> And, from her head down to her feet,
> A subtle air, a dangerous perfume
> Floats about her dusky body.

If one accepts this view, one can infer from it that the dual unity soul-body is, if not unstable, at least partial, and that the most volatile element of the being escapes relatively from the gangue around which it "swims" or "floats," held fast. The attraction which throws and breaks the poet and Jeanne both to and from each other would indeed be of a fatal nature: that of minds linked for eternity, situated together on a plane of reality of which the flesh would be only "the ephemeral ghost" (*Les Fleurs du Mal,* xxxix); a reality that intemporal memory, such as a spiritual perfume, would maintain present in spite of the ravages of time and the apparent death of love. This is a Neo-Platonistic theme, underlying many of the poems in *Les Fleurs du Mal,* and which Swedenborg illustrated as a visionary. What falls under the senses reflects a form which is imperceptible to them, itself a reflection of the Idea. In light of this conception, we shall see shortly what tie unites demon, Beauty, and woman. But now, let us observe that in the eyes of the poet the physical nature of this latter is an enigma.

> . . . In that nature, symbolic and strange,
> Where pure angel is united with ancient sphinx,
>
> (xxvii)

the body could well be the "work of some obeah, Faust of the savanna" (*Sed non satiata*), who would have created the man-woman of whom a wicked spirit makes his habitation; or of the demon himself, of whom the poet, in *La Destruction,* tells us that

> Sometimes, knowing my deep love for Art, he assumes
> The form of a most seductive woman,

in order to lead him "far from the sight of God."

Another kind of woman—feminine form rather—offers to the poet an angelic counterbalance to the demon's malice. This divine nature possesses, but with opposite qualities the same elements of feminine charm as the demoniacal nature: eyes, flame, perfume. The look of the demon is impenetrable and cutting, that of the Angel radiates and vivifies; the "torch of hell" (*Le Monstre*) is evidently the opposite of the "living torch." The latter illuminates the steps of the poet "on the pathway of Beauty": it is a *fantôme* in the sense elaborated above, a spiritual reality analogous, but in an inverse fashion, to the "elastic phantom" of the goddess, Pleasure. This emanation from the feminine being, a shadow whose body would be only the visible residue, and whose "spiritual flesh has the perfume of Angels," "dances" or "flutters" in all places beside the poet, like its antithesis, the Demon in *La Destruction*. When the Demon draws him to the cursed place of its dark solemnities, unfurling "all the bloody instruments of Destruction," the blandishments of the "Being, lucid and pure" are salutary, its love and Beauty are only one, as befits whoever can affirm:

"I am your guardian Angel, your Muse and Madonna" (XLII).

It would be easy to multiply the reversed relations between the two symbolic types of woman; this game would not be uninstructive concerning the mechanism of the symbolizing function in the author of *Les Fleurs du Mal*. In *Tout entière*, for example (where the Demon, in the "high room" or place of mystical communion, would like to induce the poet to detail minutely the ideal woman like an *object* while her adorer lives from Her and by Her in a unitary contemplation), the name which designates the devil, "the Abhorred one," is an antonym of the Adored one. Let us leave the antinomies to emphasize at least a resemblance between these two contrasting feminine figures: the poet is bound to them by a reciprocal destiny. It is true that, weakly indicated in a poem like *Le Flambeau Vivant,* where it is said about the eyes of Madame Sabatier, eyes of the Angel, "these divine brothers who are my brothers too":

They are my servitors, I am their humble slave,

this reciprocity is expressed in a manner far more convincing and terrible when it is a question of the "Accurst being," of the "tall angel with a brow of bronze," female demon incarnated by Jeanne Duval and whose Beauty under its fearful aspect is the hypostasis (*F.M.,* XXXIX). Moreover the "Accurst being" and the "Being pure, lucid" are less in opposition than in a state of inverse reciprocity: each can be called the other and yet they are mutually exclusive. Thus "memory" or the very pure "phantom" hovers "over the smoking ruins of stupid orgies." *L'Aube Spirituelle,* in which we read this line, was sent to Madame Sabatier with this prefatory declaration: "After a night of pleasure and desolation my soul belongs to you."[12] This communication, and other analogous ones, will remain anonymous for five whole years, until the appearance of *Les Fleurs du Mal.* In the meantime, Baudelaire explains this anonymity in a letter destined to give the spiritual reason for it, but which confesses the stimulus that his erotic imagination receives from it:

> Finally, to explain to you my silence, and my ardor, an ardor which is almost religious, I shall say to you that whenever my being is rolled down into the black of its natural wickedness and stupidity, it dreams deeply of you. From this exciting and purifying revery is born generally a fortunate accident.—You are for me not only the most attractive of women;—of all women, but moreover the dearest and most precious of superstitions.—I am an egoist, I use you.—Here is my wretched bumswipe[13].—How much happier I would be if I could be certain that these lofty conceptions of love have some chance of being well received in a secret corner of your adorable mind!—I shall never know (letter to Madame Sabatier, May 8, 1854).

The ambiguity—conscious or not, amorous epistolary art having many ruses—of this missive, which is almost overly revealing, is found, along with the word *superstition,* in the letter in which Baudelaire reveals his identity. Superstition must be understood in the sense that Joseph de Maistre understood it: a conviction ventured beyond beliefs considered legitimate. All idolatry, Plotinus already thought, becomes reasonable for the one who sees that there exists a sympathy between the idol and the superior force that it in fact represents. The "ardently desired and cherished image" maintains itself *above* the poet, like an Angel:

Baudelaire believes that there exists between it and himself a mysterious relationship. But in the same breath, he confesses that he uses it only for an egoistic, magical evocation: that which produces a "fortunate accident." In his letter of August 18, 1857, he will go further into this involuntary lucidity, in speaking of "this intimacy" (between him and the image) "in which I have been receiving the answer for such a long time." Less than two weeks later, the "secret corner," the "dear nook" (*Hymne*) has ceased being a mystical sanctuary: in giving herself, Madame Sabatier fell. Superstition is not faith; it is bad faith, and the letter of August 31 is full of it, in which we read a disintoxicated impotence, a misogyny through excessive idolatry, that the destiny of childhood explains if it does not justify. What an agonizing confession is that which, in an ironic tone, laments the rape of the venerable interdict and reconstructs it immediately on the human level, in expiation for the transgression on the celestial level! "And finally, finally, a few days ago, you were a deity, which is so suitable, which is so beautiful, so inviolable. Now you are just woman." Thus, in *Laquelle est la vraie?* the "Bénédicta, who filled the atmosphere with ideal," dies a few days after his meeting her, and it is another Bénédicta, identical but diabolically opposed, who revindicates, in a burst of laughter, the love of the poet as punishment for his blindness.

In the closed universe of interacting symbols that Baudelaire's erotic "spirituality" is, female Angel and female Demon appear like the front and back sides of one and the same aberrant, grandiose psychic formation, "femininity" both abyssal and impenetrable. Whether she be Angel or Demon, never does the poet converse with woman. He soliloquizes in her presence and even in her place, sometimes; he addresses to himself with her mouth the words that he wants to hear; but let her attempt to express herself and he immediately suggests that she be silent. And to affirm then that woman is a "terrible and incommunicable being like God (with this difference that infinity does not communicate itself because it would blind and crush the finite, whereas the being of whom we speak is perhaps incomprehensible only because it has nothing to communicate)" (*A.R.,* 93). "Divinity," "star," "idol, stupid perhaps" but "frightful," a rival of God in that she is "for most men, the source of the keenest, and even, let us say it shamefully, of philosophical voluptuousness, of the most lasting pleasures, the creature toward whom or to the profit of whom go all their efforts" (*A.R.,* 93), woman is then essentially a formidable object of cult, mystical or sexual or both according to a sacred ambivalence. This cult has two poles which exclude each other: the one esoteric, the passion for the mother; the other exoteric, the inverse attachment to Jeanne. Between the two are some figures lending to equivocal mysticities, which, for a time, suspend the erotic vertigo and the maternal interdict. But these are mirages quickly dissipated, caricatures of the tendency. Baudelaire's spirituality is in the fall: his religion—for it is one, even if he has in part fabricated it for himself departing from an initial fatality—consists of falling from forbidden love into culpable sexuality, of refusing the soul to the one and the flesh to the other. The celestial idol and the infernal idol are two statues of the same refusal, guardians of a single repressed misfortune.

Clandestine part of most human existences, often disguised or repudiated, the erotic cult takes the thousand shapes of the interrupted dream. Its major symbol is seen everywhere, calling for universal promiscuity: "Two fine immortal religions, on the walls, eternal obsessions of the people: a prick (the antique phallus)—and 'Long live Barbès!' or 'Down with Philippe!' or 'Long live the Republic!'" (*J.I.,* 92). The beautiful dream described to Asselineau shows us to what extent subsconscious elaboration magnifies the primitive symbolism and reinforces the archaic magic of it as a basis for prohibition. The poet's merit—

influenced by the *black* libertinage of the preceding century—is to have given a name to this cult: that of *counterreligion*. In his *Conseils aux jeunes littérateurs* (1846) he expresses his indignation at seeing "a pack of poets made dull by pagan pleasures, and who use endlessly the words *saint, ecstasy, prayer,* etc., to qualify things and creatures that have nothing saintly or ecstatic about them, but rather to the contrary, extending thus the adoration of woman to the most disgusting degree of impiety. One of them, in an excess of *saintly* eroticism, went to the point of crying: o my *Catholic* mistress! One might as well smear excrement on an altar" (*A.R.,* 282). He, however, gave himself over to this systematic sacrilege. See how he celebrates Sara la Louchette, and the sexual inversion that he begins thus (*Œ.P.,* I, 13):

> In silence do I lick her with more fervor
> Than the burning Madeleine the Savior's feet.

But he gives way to this blasphemous liturgy with full knowledge of what it is. Anatole France is right in saying that "his best verses are inspired by the old prose of the Church and by the hymns of the breviary," applied to a completely different object. *Franciscae meae Laudes* is more than a parody: it is, more than *Hymne* or *Tout entière,* an example of countermystique, expressed, like a defiance, in the language of medieval spirituality. From the *Stabat Mater* (*Eia Mater fons amoris*) [See the Mother, source of love] and from the *Dies Irae* (*Salva me fons pietatis*) [Save me, fount of piety] derive the two verses: "Piscina plena virtutis,/Fons aeternae juventutis" [Reservoir full of virtue,/Fountain of eternal youth]. Likewise the "Sicut beneficum Lethe, Hauriam oscula de te, Quae imbuta es magnete" [As from a benign Lethe,/I shall drink kisses from you,/Who were given a magnet's strength] suggests the hymn *Induant justitiam,* which is sung on Assumption Day: "Hauris unde plenior, Hoc e fonte crebior, Stillet in nos gratia" [Whence you drink more heartily, more frequently from this spring, may grace be instilled in us]. The theme of regeneration: "Quod erat spurcum, cremasti; Quod rudius, exaequasti; Quod debile, confirmasti," [You have burned that which was filthy,/Made smooth that which was rough,/Strengthened that which was weak] is patterned after the stanza of *Veni sancte Spiritus:* "Lava quod est sordidum, Riga quod est aridum, Sana quod est saucium" [Wash that which is unclean, Water that which is dry, Heal that which is injured]. Finally, the concluding allusion to the bread and wine of the sacrament signals the counterreligious intent: "Panis salsus, mollis esca, Divinum vinum, Francisca!" [Bread seasoned with salt, delectable dish,/Heavenly wine—My Frances]. This consecration of the black mass could be compared to the evocation of Eros-Satan holding in his right hand a vial filled with a red liquid and labeled with these strange words: "Drink, this is my blood, a perfect cordial" (*Les Tentations, P.P.P.*).

The "seminarian's jargon" that Samuel uses in the presence of La Fanfarlo, who was "accustomed to this mystical language, mixed with impurities and with terrible crudities," is, to be sure, a fad of the times; for the poet of *Les Fleurs du Mal,* it is a part of a regenerative ritual. It is, unconsciously, an incessant evocation to the Mother, *de profundis,* from the depths of the "tomb," the "dungeon," the "prison," the "hovel," into which the poet has been cast by life. *A une Madone* can be read simultaneously on several levels; but the "underground altar" that he builds for her "in the depths of [his] distress," the niche "in the blackest corner of [his] heart," similar to the omnipresent memory "on the tenebrous background of [his] soul" (*Confession*), is this not the secret of a nostalgia ineffable except under a disguise? He purposely makes this "Mortal Madonna" play the "role of Mary," the Virgin-Mother, *Regina,* "triumphant Queen, fecund in redemptions," trampling beneath her feet the serpent which "is eating the heart" of her antichrist son, the poet. Strangely, the barbaric

Stabat at the end of the poem corresponds to the notes of hate in *Bénédiction*. It is indeed the Mother of the Seven Sorrows, in truth as in caricature, that is injured by the conscience while rending itself, whereby Baudelaire, "torturer full of remorse," makes a profession in evil. And in the line "Taking your deepest love for a target," the ambiguity of the possessive, in a single sacrificial image, unites in one Heart the mother and the son as if, in her, it was he aiming at himself:

> I love you Marie, that cannot be denied; but the love that I feel for you is that of the Christian for his God; therefore never give a terrestrial and often shameful name to this incorporeal and mysterious cult, to this sweet and chaste attraction that joins my soul to yours, in spite of your will. That would be a sacrilege.—I was dead, and you have brought me back to life. . . . Henceforth, you are my unique queen, my passion and my beauty; you are the part of me that a spiritual essence has formed (*Correspondence,* I, 103).

This famous passage from a letter to Marie Daubrun would be only an epistolary ecstasy, a "beautiful lie" offered up again in identical terms to Madame Sabatier, if these too angelicized creatures were for Baudelaire anything except a pretext to release "this part of [himself] that a spiritual essence has formed." And that, in order to prostitute it then to the sacrilegious pseudo-Madonna:

> Under your satin slippers,
> Under your dear silken feet,
> I place all my happiness,
> My genius and destiny,
>
> My soul brought to life by you,
> By your clear light and color,
> Explosion of heat
> In my dark Siberia!
>   [*Chanson d'après-midi.*]

All Baudelaire's poetic work expresses, and accomplishes in the imagination, an operation of sacrificial metamorphosis which is rather easy to define: he is brought back to life to be destroyed, he is destroyed in order to be brought back to life; woman is both the instrument of this resurrection and the abyss of this fall. She is, at once, the metamorphosing force, the place of the metamorphosis, and the metamorphosed reality—a mystical All, reflected infinitely in her correspondences and of whom the poet is prisoner as much as worshiper. From this tender and ferocious fatality, he draws, it must be said "with what diabolical care," a pleasure regenerated on a real background of definitive claustration and ennui. Dead-living, closed up in woman as though in a sepulchre or a well, even when he is "saturated with intoxicating delights" from it, he "longs for suffering," like Tannhaüser, like the only absolute dimension that a sequestered person is capable of. What he expects from woman is, through her, to be reborn endlessly to sorrow and grief and pain, to utter in the process the "sublime cry." And the creature who gives birth to him by expulsing him, creates him by refusing him, is represented in reality by woman, ideally by Beauty.

> Accurst being to whom, from the deep abysm
> To the highest heaven, nothing responds, save me!
> —O you who, like an ephemeral ghost,
>
> Trample lightly and with a serene look
> Upon the dull mortals who found you repugnant,
> Jet eyed statue, tall angel with a brow of bronze!
> ["*Je te donne ces vers. . . .*"]

Woman "carries out a kind of duty by striving to appear magic and supernatural"; the abstract unity obtained from rice powder "immediately makes the human being appear to be closer to the statue, that is to a divine and superior being"; the made-up eye, which does not see but captivates, is a "window open upon infinity"; rouge "adds to a beautiful feminine face the mysterious passion of the priestess" (*A.R.*, 99). Thus adorned, a living statue that the most beautiful pages of *Les Fleurs du Mal* celebrate, woman is Beauty itself. Their mutual ambivalence is resolved, in *Hymne à la Beauté,* by the identity of opposites. To the question asked four times in various forms: "Do you come from heaven or rise from the abyss?" there is only their reciprocal, enigmatic evidence for an answer. This "mysterious Sphinx," this "nature, symbolic and strange," woman or Beauty, rules all, and singularly the thought of the poet, according to an arbitrariness which "pours out confusedly benevolence and crime"— such is the Demon of *La Destruction.* The poet is personally bound to this *cursed* Creature by an erotic destiny ("Destiny, bewitched, follows your skirts like a dog"), oriented, through the female, toward the return to the forbidden womb, and, no doubt, to primitive unity. Because this destiny seems to pass death and perpetuate itself in successive lives, as we shall try to show in studying the theme of *le Gouffre,* The Abyss. In echo to the great apostrophe cited earlier, addressed as much to Jeanne Duval as to the supernatural essence that she represents, here is a vision of eternal Beauty, purveyor of Death if not Death itself, a vision in which phallic symbolism is not absent:

> You walk upon corpses which you mock, O Beauty!
> Of your jewels Horror is not the least charming,
> And Murder, among your dearest trinkets,
> Dances amorously upon your proud belly.
> [*Hymne à la Beauté.*]

One inexhaustibly mysterious poem, *La Mort des Artistes,* sheds definite symbolic light on the unitary metamorphosis of woman, Beauty and Death. It evokes first, so it seems, the ritual already cited in *L'Examen de Minuit,* the kiss of stupid matter, the devil's rear end: a ritual performed each day, from life to life perhaps.

> How many times must I shake my bauble and bells
> And kiss your low forehead, dismal caricature?
> To strike the target of mystic nature.
> How many javelins must I waste, O my quiver?
> [*La Mort des Artistes.*]

This "dismal caricature," "the stupid matter" of *L'Examen de Minuit,* is the antithesis, but also the deformed material image of "the glorious Creature" (the "ideal face" in the first version of the sonnet), "for whom infernal desire makes our hearts grieve." Without a doubt, because of the act that it describes, a directly sexual interpretation of this quatrain could be made. It would be then an image of impotence to effect the penetration or reintegration "of mystical nature," an obscure but expressive variant of which is "mystical quadrature." Such an impotence is due spiritually to the fall, one aspect of which is degradation, caricatural deformation of matter, *mater,* in Sanskrit *mâtrâ,* the measure of all things (René Guénon, *Le Règne de la Quantité*). In the symbolism of Tradition, at the lowest level of the solidification of the world, the wheel of this latter ceases to turn, becomes square. This "mystical quadrature" marks the end of an eon of time, and the restoration to the primordial state through transcendent intervention. Thus we understand that this "dream carved in stone," Beauty

> Is made to inspire in the poet a love
> As eternal and silent as matter.

A sorrowful love, a distillation of a suffering which is more and more indispensable, and of which the fall, paradoxically, would seemingly be the "eternal alembic," thanks to which the spirit is refined. The first version of the poem gave a glimpse of a refuge in death which "good nature" offers. Nothing like this is apparent in the definitive version, which does not conjecture any end to fatality. The real end would be unity with it, contemplation of "the glorious Creature," of superior Beauty, independent of the passions linked to the fall, and which, perhaps, is for each *Monos* its *Una,* for each one of us, his being completely regenerated. "The ideal is not this vague thing, this weary and impalpable dream which floats around the ceilings of academies;—an ideal is the individual rectified by the individual, reconstructed and returned by the brush or the chisel to the dazzling truth of his original harmony" (*C.E.,* 143–144). Reintegrated, how? By dint of pursuing the ideal in its mortal images, in two apparently opposite directions, the high and the low, heaven and the abyss, the "austere study" of the poet and the devastating "labors" of the debauchee. Whence the ambivalence of the "infernal desire," concupiscence inherent in the fall but connected to redemptive grief by nostalgia which increases as the fallen creature falls. The fall itself, although irremediable, can, from the fact of this active orientation that consciousness in evil represents, change, *not in nature, but in an intimate sense,* and the degradation is integrated in the expiation. In the first version, this degradation is only of the body: it is a shaping of filth, perhaps of the "vile animal," of this "queen of sin" which nature uses "to fashion a genius." In the definitive version, it is the soul which is worn away "in subtle schemes," no doubt aided by the "crafty accomplice," Satan, the Prince and protector of the exiled and the evicted,

> . . . who teaches through love the taste for Heaven
> To the cursed pariah, even to the leper.
> [*Les Litanies de Satan.*]

This wearing away of the soul—slow *annihilation-reintegration* —is it done through the laborious suffering of art, the creative force of works which are so many sketches and gangues whose destruction is the indispensable corollary of their creation? Or, on the contrary, does the soul become exhausted in an erotic pursuit of which the seized object is the opposite of the creature imagined? Or else does this interminable labor of the fall continue in the series of reincarnations, and does it overcome, one after the other, "many a heavy armature," "the human armature" designating the skeleton (*Danse macabre*), and then the edifice of the body?

The haphazard quest of the darkness, according to the laws of a fatality escaping whoever submits to it, will it open, as the poet wishes to believe (*Hymne à la Beauté*), the door of

An infinity I love but have not ever known?

The exemplary image, the *Idole,* by which and through which "the soul perceives splendors situated beyond the tomb" (*A.R.*), remains ignored by its worshipers no matter what images they create of them. Under the myth of incommunicability peculiar to woman and to art, the Mother was thus, for the poet of *Les Fleurs du Mal,* the great paradisiac Unknown. An intolerably grievous Unknown element, the sign of an infinite loss. "Sculptors damned and branded with shame," forgers of ideal approximations "go pounding on their chests and brows," in other words, working on themselves, taking themselves as raw material and as object with a creative furor born from remorse and aspiration. Destroying themselves to attain their essence, they put their ultimate hope, "bizarre and sombre Capitol!," in a Death which will be perhaps for them only a new precipitation from the summit of the rock of the ideal. The "flowers of their brains" which they expect to open beyond the grave, these *flowers of evil,* "death-like chrysalids" (*Le Flacon*), which have not blossomed in the limbo of earthly life, will they open up in the bosom of Death, inverted and frightful image of the Mother, and which, in the final apostrophe of *Le Voyage,* is another name for Beauty? Or else, are these earthly flowers only the testimony of a past life whose secret, evoked enigmatically by their perfume, is lost in an unfathomable nostalgia? (*Le Guignon.*) These are questions that we have been faced with on the brink of the gulf whose psychic nature we have tried to explore and which we are going to demonstrate is, at quite different depths, a spiritual abyss.

III. Aesthetic Spirituality

1. The Mystique of the Gulf

Erotic tenderness in *Les Fleurs du Mal* is a ritual of idealization or of recollection; the sexual embrace precipitates degradation and oblivion. But their antinomy is only apparent: neither tenderness nor pleasure is a form of amorous plenitude; both accentuate nostalgia and duality. These are two phases, two *postulations,* of a single symbolic act, erotic and spiritual. Sexual love is the gulf; platonic love is memory. Each is the complement of the other that it contains like a negation or a mirage: the Angel awakens the somber appetite of rape; the Demon, the vertigo of unity. It is in fact that a single way is opened to the creature: the fall, which separates ever further from an origin which cannot be known, but which stimulates thus in reverse, in the mind attentive by essence, the faculty—the magic will—of recalling for eternity what time destroys without hope of return.

Poem xxiv is, in ten lines, one of the most powerful illustrations of this dialectic of the imaginary. "Implacable and cruel beast," woman is likewise a "vase of sadness": *machine* (as in the following poem), and *form* or receptacle of an essence, of this "fathomless gloom" which is the "gulf we may not sound"—"the nocturnal vault," but engulfed. The adoration goes less to heaven itself, by the intermediary of its inverted image, than to this image considered as inverse of heaven, and by opposition to it. Woman is only the mortal cover of the Being which has destroyed in itself the image of Heaven. For this Being which inhabits them and metamorphoses them at its will, the soul and the feminine body are only instruments which believe themselves to be free: they

> Insolently use a borrowed power
> Without ever knowing the law of their beauty.

As for the Creature from which this power comes to them, he has for his congener "the camel of Cazotte—camel, devil and woman." The infernal "Beatrice" of the poet resembles this Biondetta of the *Diable amoureux,* whom Alvare, under orders, calls "Spirit which is bound to a body only for me, and for me alone." We have already pointed out this correspondence or reciprocal predestination uniting for eternity

> Like two angels who are tortured
> By a relentless delirium,
>   (*Le Vin des Amants.*)

two *spirits* spurring each other on in a hellish frenzy. Mutual vampirism, which mysteriously harmonizes with the one that each vampire inflicts upon itself, by reason of its never ending covetousness.

These two vampires, these two spirits, are then each at work on the other. While man, in the arms of woman, is sucked toward a terrible hollow heaven by the silent spirit in her, he himself bustles around mentally, through a sinister emulation, in this voluptuous alchemy of the carrion whose aim is constant in

Baudelaire, whether he practices it on the dead one or the live one: to evoke, beginning with the exterior covering, by an attentive distillation of all the senses, the creature in its very essence, the form that memory at once apprehends and subtilizes. What form? What identity? That, perhaps, of a common incorruptible reality, to be two and one, the memory of which—evanescent osmosis—suggests the desire and the trace. Thus the theme of the carrion, be it woman (*Une Charogne, Une Martyre*) or man (*Le Vampire, Un Voyage à Cythère*), is confused with its apparent opposite, the infinite quest for spiritual unity. That which is tomb, decay, is also gulf, essence. In such a manner a spiritual ether, "a whole far-away world, absent, almost defunct," is born from the vile greed of vermin, which is a symbol of limitless dissociation, multiplication.

The same logic, in *Duellum,* drives two forces equally voracious, to clutch together and exterminate each other, as they roll toward the abyss to be eternalized. Two opposed movements, one of sublimation, the other of fall, call out and respond to each other; to the eternally distant, there corresponds like a mirror time which is without end—a dialectic analogous to that of the return to the forbidden womb and of the forbidden return to the womb. Thus unity forever lost becomes the *integral* of memory and of the fall: he who knows that he falls, remembers, and vice versa. Fall and memory are one and the same act that two beings formally separated accomplish, each for himself, in the act of love. Bound by a sempiternal fatality, they are, however, incommunicable between themselves. Two twin solipsisms: such is the amorous relation for Baudelaire. Never does the poet show how, in their reciprocal predestination, Jeanne Duval can use him; on the other hand, *Les Fleurs du Mal* shows us the use he makes of her, as the image of a nostalgia and an instrument of a vengeance.

In a similar ecstasy,
My sister, floating side by side,
We'll flee without ever stopping
To the paradise of my dreams!
[*Le Vin des Amants.*]

It may be that Baudelaire found this conception of amorous dualism in the works of Joseph de Maistre. The author of the *Soirées* goes further, seeing in the sexual combat an aspect of the cosmic struggle between two wills which penetrate each other and in which each strives toward its end, reintegration for one, pursuit of division for the other. Love partakes of these two powers: man "wants to be two" in it, but likewise wants to join himself to one other than himself. It is true that the *other,* with Baudelaire, is not subject but object, pretext for emergence from oneself, and not the coauthor of a new symbol of union. "The troublesome thing in love is that it is a crime in which one must have an accomplice" (*J.I.,* 74). What crime? The fall itself. Sexual love is "a joy of descending." Its finality is not in pleasure, but in the aggravation of the fall and the increasing lucidity of the fallen spirit.

> The satanic titillations of a vague sensuality are soon succeeded by impulsive movements, swoonings, cries of victory, moans of gratitude, and then howls of ferocity, the reproachful cries of the victims and the impious hosannas of their sacrificers, as if savagery must always find a place in the drama of love and the enjoyment of the flesh must always lead, by some ineluctable Satanic logic, to the ecstatic delights of crime (*A.R., Richard Wagner,* 222).

It is the tone of *Duellum;* to "puling love," of an unconscious ferocity, succeeds the unintentional "fury of mature hearts." According to Swedenborg, hell is populated with spirits which are nothing more than human souls having chosen vice, for eternity.

Let me take repose in love.—But no—love will not give me rest. Candor and goodness are disgusting. If you wish to please me and rejuvenate my passion, be cruel, deceitful, libertine, and thieving; and if you do not want to be that, I shall strike you down without anger. For I am the true representative of irony, and my malady is of a kind that is absolutely incurable[1] (letter to V. de Mars, April 7, 1855).

This endlessly reiterated choice gives grandeur to love such as Baudelaire understands it: not closed in a narrow mutual possession, but open by the wound of irony, goaded by vice, and constantly renewed by *prostitution*.

This last word, under Baudelaire's pen, is a model of ambivalence which governs all his symbolism. In a letter of his eighteenth year, Baudelaire displays his enthusiasm over "something which lifts me up, what do I mean? a violent desire to embrace all." This is a movement apparently centrifugal which, as Crépet and Blin have noted, projects out to everything and to anybody, not through charity, but through an intoxication which can become vertigo. "Power to expand into infinity" is inverted in "a dark abyss of human pollution": the "insatiable *I* of the *non-I*"[2] (*A.R.*) assumes total consciousness of the fall; it exalts itself and degrades itself purposely, so as to revive in itself this consciousness. Whence, in the pity which is at once cosmic and narcissic that forms the basis of Baudelairian lucidity, the importance of sight, the eye, where "the wearisome spectacle of immortal sin" inscribes itself. *The eye is a whore,* says the English proverb; but Baudelaire, "corrupt to the point of heroism" (Bourget), lets his eye, drawn toward the chasm wander over everything, deepening things only to be drawn in. The one who saw a *counterreligion,* a *satanic religion,* in "the sacred prostitution" to which his soul surrenders, felt, inversely, with no less justice, that "the most prostituted creature is the creature par excellence, God, since he is the supreme companion for each individual, since he is the common inexhaustible reservoir of love" (*J.I.,* 79–80). An additional text can be compared to that one, in which lingers no doubt the mustiness of emanatism, and which strangely brings together Satan and God, since it implies in divine love this mysterious "joy of descending," this attraction toward the bottom from which its human counterpart derives: "What is the fall? If it is unity become duality, it is God who has fallen. In other words, would not the creation be the fall of God?" (*J.I.,* 73).

In the poet's dynamics, what is the *fall?* It is first of all, by intermediary of the imagination and the senses, the symbolic translation of the traumatisms undergone by the child, including perhaps that mysterious one of his coming into the world. To fall is to be expelled from the womb. In *Bénédiction* Baudelaire accuses the mother of this dethronement. But, in the same moment, he absolves her of it: "the eternal designs" require that the mother and the son be each for the other instruments of expiation. It remains that the "outcast Child" will never admit his frustration, and will perpetuate his royal exile during his entire adult life. Resentment and necessity will impose upon him "the repression of all expansion." Whence his incurable solitude: in *Irrémédiable* and *Rêve parisien,* two supreme moments—one of elevation, the other of fall—identically resolved, the poet is alone "in the depths of a vast nightmare," in a "silence of eternity." And more than alone: in the two instances, he discovers anew what he already knows—that he is his own sepulcher.

> ——My soul is a tomb where, bad cenobite,
> I wander and dwell eternally;
>   (*Le Mauvais Moine.*)

Not only is this life completely dead, and the tomb the antonym of the womb, but, by symbolic extrapolation, the soul, place of successive existences (and of universal compassion) is the *change* which outlives every change, the meta-temporal gangue of the being. To fall is in a sense, by the acceleration of the fall, to become more and more conscious of this soul in its opaqueness, of its immobility, of the inertia which increases with consciousness itself. The fall is both indefinitely accelerated and indefinitely retarded: likewise time, that of *L'Horloge* marking each second, that of the Fates eternally unwinding the thread (*De profundis clamavi*).

These contradictory symbols represent an almost permanent state that the poet does not cease describing. Already Cramer, in *La Fanfarlo,* suffers from "debauchery of the spirit, [from] impotence of the heart, which means that the one lives now only out of curiosity, and the other dies each day from lassitude" (*P.A.,* 250) Baudelaire's letters to his mother are filled with accusations against himself which turn against her, and whose sole cause is the vicious circle of idleness: "Imagine a perpetual idleness made necessary by a perpetual malaise, with a deep hatred for this idleness, and the impossibility of escaping it, because of the perpetual lack of money" (December 4, 1847). A lack of money which is evidently the symbol of another lack for which the mother is held responsible, and of an otherwise serious asphyxia. Having received Méryon's visit, Baudelaire wonders why he himself who has "always had in mind and temperament all that was required to go insane" has not done so. He owes it doubtlessly to his "hysterical" nature, in the sense this word had in his time: "The doctor says: hysteria! hysteria! You must convince yourself, you must make yourself walk" (letter to his mother, February 10, 1866). This constraint he imposed upon himself by an aggravating conscience, which made him intractable and contributed to breaking him. In a letter to Charles Asselineau, he describes in an impressive manner his attacks, which are so many episodes of his fall: tumbles, vomitings, sweat, stupor, "that invariably is the gradation." What he said of E. A. Poe, "he had forever disgusting difficulties to overcome," applies equally to himself.

The poetic representation of these difficulties is more eloquent than their clinical description. And without a doubt, in transposing them to the spiritual plane, the representation gives the true reason for them: neurosis is here a destiny. A careful reading of *Les Fleurs du Mal* furnishes both a symptomatology of the fall and the range of correspondences owing to which Baudelaire *plays* with his malady or rather awakens by it a salutary and sorrowful secret. He must feel physically—how does one escape it?—efforts, gestures, the coenesthesia of the poet in his word, in order, himself, to approach this secret from within:

> I, my soul is flawed, and when, a prey to ennui,
> She wishes to fill the cold night air with her songs,
> It often happens that her weakened voice
>
> Resembles the death rattle of a wounded man,
> Forgotten beneath a heap of dead, by a lake of blood,
> Who dies without moving, striving desperately.
>   (*La Cloche Fêlée.*)

Here, each important word contributes to the overall symbolism and refers to the entire system of Baudelairian images, to his spiritual universe. Thus the flaw in the soul, which corresponds to the original blemish. This "wounded man, forgotten . . . , by a lake of blood," which attests expiation and vengeance (de Maistre would call this latter "the occult and terrible law that requires human blood"), is the creature who never finishes with punishment, and whose every existence is a new effort, adding to, instead of alleviating, the weight of his past lives: so that the increasing solidification of the will to live goes in pace with the useless mobilization of the will to die. *La Cloche Fêlée* echoes *Le Guignon,* a strange poem composed of two fragments translated from Longfellow and from Thomas Gray, and yet so Baudelairian. But *Le Guignon* points to a secret buried beneath the weight of the individual, the weight that Sisyphus, from life to life, is condemned, and knows himself to be incapable, to bear. We shall see further on the theme of the secret; let us retain here only the image of Sisyphus, the man who enchained the spirit of Death sent by God to kill him. The punishment inflicted upon Sisyphus was because of his impiety, because in binding up Thanatos, he made himself the accuser of God. Likewise Baudelaire, when he refuses "the conditions of life," which is tantamount to precipitating it into the absurd and imputing God with the responsibility of the fall. Such is the mechanism of the *hysteria of the mind,* of the melancholia which Kierkegaard defined in a manner the poet would have readily found acceptable: "Melancholia is the sin and more precisely the sin *instar omnium,* for not expressing the will to the depths of one's being is sinning, and this deficiency is the source of all sins" (*L'Alternative*).

Initial refusal, archaic, intensively lived by Baudelaire who, in order to justify it, draws from it the elements of a cosmogony. By all means, including art and magic, man has always tried to flee, "even if it were only a few hours, his habitation of filth" (*P.A.,* 5). This one, the cave of Empedocles, matter, flesh, nature—is a "leaden, miry Styx," "a gloomy world with a leaden horizon" made so by "a black and miry sky." In short, hell itself, a place of eternal nonlife and nondeath: a place also of the partially formed, of mire. According to Swedenborg, the fall causes harmful creatures to be born; detached from God, men and their thoughts "become forms of hell and, therefore, forms of the demon" (*Vera christiana Religio*). Likewise, Baudelaire believed "that maleficent and despicable animals were perhaps only the vivification, the corporification, the manifestation of the wicked thoughts of man. Thus all of *nature* participates in the original sin" (letter to Toussenel, January 21, 1856). Creation is, therefore, an evil; at the end of the eighteenth century, many thinkers believed this firmly, de Maistre among them ("evil has spoiled everything, and man in his entirety is only a malady"), and Sade ("I have a horror of nature, which does nothing except evil"). Sade invites one through disgust and defiance, to be Nature's rival in the abominable, whereas de Maistre never "meditates on this frightful subject without being tempted to throw [himself] to the ground like a guilty man who calls for mercy"; their contradictory attitudes have their synthesis in Baudelaire, martyr and torturer, victim and sacrificer.

This *héautontimorouménos,* or self-torturer, guilty and avenger of himself, is in the image of the *One,* alienated from the emanatist myths: in *La Fontaine de sang,* the poet is identified with the Absolute, bleeding upon the world and yet without wound, a paradox which, in fact, is formed at the root of all metaphysics where the One leaves itself and *prostitutes itself* in the creation. How does the One remain intact while its blood, under the effect of a mysterious original attack, is spread upon "each creature" so as to slake his thirst and mark him? Is formal creation represented by this blood which never stops flowing? (*Blood,* in the Semitic tradition, symbolizes the Spirit.) What is certain is that in Baudelaire's eyes the infinite effusion into multiplicity has as its driving force *love,* for agents those creatures who experience love and arouse it: but blood thus distributed carries an increasing suffering, a power of malediction as much as salvation. After de Maistre, this vision astonishes Baudelaire, who, all his life, will vainly seek the means "to lay to rest for a single day the terror which consumes [him]." For if suffering is ambivalent to this degree, necessary as much as fatal, man cannot not do evil, and has the choice only of being victim or demiurge of his degradation: as God, in parallel fashion, according to de Maistre, is the author of the evil that punishes, not of the evil that sullies.

In consenting to God's justice, "in place of being only patients, we shall be at least victims," says de Maistre again. There is a third choice, that—theoretical—of Sade: to go one better than malediction in the name of freedom, and become more wicked than nature. If Baudelaire makes none of these choices, and if he opts for the double role of victim and of torturer, the fault is in his cosmogony, and especially in his poetic nature. His terror, while at the same time his delight, is *the fall;* that is to say, life in its principle, like sempiternal hell: place of eternity and yet of passage, the *hostelry of punishment,* so well named by De Quincey. This latter, Baudelaire tells us,

> affirms that if life could magically open up before us, if our eye, still young, could wander through the corridors, scrutinize the halls and chambers of this hostelry, theaters of the future trage- dies which await us, we and our friends would draw back, trembling in horror (*P.A.,* 195).

One remembers that the same De Quincey draws back in a similar fashion before the secret of birth, an episode, doubtlessly, of the eternal horror that he senses. Baudelaire borrows the hostel image from him, to apply, with a startling ambivalence, some- times to the repose of death which cannot be found ("The Devil has put out all the lights at the inn!"), sometimes to the insatiable eternity of Hate:

> Hatred is a drunkard in a tavern,
> Who feels his thirst grow greater with each drink
> And multiply itself like the Lernaean hydra.
> (*Le Tonneau de la Haine.*)

This sonnet, which deserves a careful analysis because in it the poet has summarized the entire operation of the fall, proves once again that Baudelaire imagines this fall in eternity. The Danaïdes have replaced Sisyphus, but that same time is multiplied and canceled endlessly. "This river which is crossed only once; the Danaïdes' cask, *always* full and *always* empty, this liver of Tityus, *always* being regenerated beneath the beak of the vulture which devours it constantly; always ready to drink this water, to seize this fruit which always escapes; this stone of Sisyphus always rolled back up, or pursued; the circle, eternal symbol of eternity, written upon Ixion's wheel . . . ," all the myths brought together here by Joseph de Maistre illustrate a single fact of spiritual experience: the reiteration of celestial punishment by the indefatigable hatred of the self. This vampirism of self-punishment, which Baudelaire has remarkably observed in himself, leads to one of the haunting images of this work, that of an irreversible sempiternity of suffering, deriving from an automatism of concupiscence which death itself does not stop: witness *Le Squelette laboureur,* or this other carcass that an "old desire" spurs and drives on, "credulous one toward Pleasure's sabbath." Witness especially, in *Le Tonneau de la Haine,* the identification of Vengeance with the sorceress Erichtho, who, by resurrecting them so as to bleed them again, forces the dead to reveal the future to her. It is from this inexhaustible blood, sempiternally shed, that Hate quickens its eternal thirst. As for the Demon, an image of tireless concupiscence, the holes that he makes in the "cask" of destiny are renewed desires which cause to move down through existence after existence the creature fallen to the power of life.

> The Demon makes secret holes in this abyss,
> Whence would escape a thousand years of sweat and strain,
> Even if she could revive her victims,
> Could bleed their bodies again, to squeeze them dry once more.
> (*Le Tonneau de la Haine,* 3rd ed., 1868.)

If the fall is still a concept, the gulf, on the other hand, is a condition. The sonnet which has *Le Gouffre* for its title is the perfect expression of it. Against a background of physiological and psychic anguish—the origin of which, we have seen, could be an incognizable childhood *trauma,* itself a symbol of a completely different rupture—a spiritual entity grows until it is identified with the fact of existing.

> —Alas! all is abysmal—action, desire, dream,
> Word!

The three words: "action, desire, dream" are placed in ascending order, in inverse order of the first line of *L'Irrémédiable:* "An Idea, a Form, a Being," a Neoplatonistic ellipsis of the Fall. The return toward the One is then as abyssal as degradation in matter: abyssal likewise is the Word, an ensemble of analogical relations, a symbol unifying all. Constantly the creature is returned to chaos by the decree of a "mocking God," with "clever hands," who paints—or what is the same—condemns to paint— (cf. *Un Fantôme, Les Ténèbres*) "an unending nightmare of many forms, place of an endless descent. Thus the spirit is ordered to nothing except the fall, whose principle is interior to it and makes it fall wherever it directs, "up, down, everywhere." Such is Baudelaire's infinity, linked, as with the Greeks, to chaos. Compare it to that of Pascal, whose gulf the poet evokes: "It is a sphere whose center is everywhere, whose circumference nowhere. In short, it is the greatest comprehensible character of the omnipotence of God that our imagination is lost in this concept." To be lost in adoration, and not, like Baudelaire, in this terror that is Promethean pride with its meaning changed.

> I tried in vain to find
> The middle and the end of space;
> I know not under what fiery eye
> I feel my pinions breaking;
> (*Les Plaintes d'un Icare.*)

A new Icarus, he will not even know the posthumous glory of his model, who gave his name to the Icarian Sea: because the gulf which opens up to him is within him, it is his being beyond all identity, across the series of existences.

In the language of heraldry, abyss is synonymous with *heart*. Often also in Baudelaire, who favors this word to the point of using it a hundred forty-two times in *Les Fleurs du Mal,* always to designate the being in his center, the principle of unity, of identity, the place of indestructible memory: and, of course, the organ of love, this other noun which is heavily weighted for Baudelaire. This center is *tantamount to being* an abyss: a vortex oriented toward the bottom. "The stairway of vertigo down which his soul plunges" (*Sur le Tasse en Prison*) signifies the ascendancy of somber powers which mount at their will "the mysterious stairway through which Hell lays seige to the weakness of man who sleeps, and communicates secretly with him" (*Les Tentations, P.P.P.*). One thinks of Saint Martin, in *L'Homme de désir*: "Learn here a secret both immense and terrible. Heart of man, you are the only outlet through which the river of deceit and death daily enters upon the earth. You are the only way through which the poisonous serpent lifts his ambitious head and through which his eyes enjoy even some rudimentary light, for his prison is indeed quite beneath ours."

Matter is this prison for bad spirits, who could really be, as in Swedenborg, human beings fallen to the level of demons, and capable of taking possession of human faculties: "This abyss is hell, thronged with our friends!" (*Duellum*). Beginning even with the preliminary *Au Lecteur,* Baudelaire plunges us into a mass of bad presences, "a legion of Demons" living off us by decree in a sense. But "swarms of ghosts . . . swirling " (*Sur Le Tasse en Prison*) are only "human miasmas" obscuring the depths of the gulf; when their whirling has caused one to lose his footing, the spirit is confused with its absolute fall, dark, silent and frozen immobility. As long as there remains a recourse (*De profundis clamavi*), the horror is not total; it is so when no hope restrains the fall in *Le Goût du Néant:*

> And Time engulfs me minute by minute,
> As the immense snow a stiffening corpse;
> I survey from above the roundness of the globe
> And I no longer seek there the shelter of a hut.
> [*Obsession.*]

The spirit strangely aspires to enjoy the perfect horror as it does its integral mirror and its pure antithesis: the real object of its desire is the primordial muteness of matter before all form, this "love eternal and silent" repressed for eternity. Thus the abyss of the heart, the vertiginous spiral of the heart, could—mysterious alembic—cause the top and bottom to communicate in a double movement and one of elevation and of fall. To seek "the empty, the black, the bare," is that not to strive for the highest through the lowest, to endeavor to analyze every name and form by exhausting the indefinite multiplicity of forms? To accomplish, by an apparently inverse asceticism, the catharsis defined by the mystics: "As long as man does not return to the state of purity which was his when he departed from his origin and passed from the uncreated state to the state of the created, he will never return unto God" (Tauler, *Sermon* XLIV). An apparently vain ambition, as *Obsession* bears witness. "Our cursed hearts, rooms of endless mourning where old deathrattles sound," do not open upon the uncreated abyss, but upon the gulf—perhaps painted? (Cf. *Un fantôme*)—of our successive lives, thick with the specters that we were, or which are eternally bound to us:

> . . . the darkness is itself a canvas
> Upon which live, springing from my eyes by thousands,
> Beings with understanding looks, who have vanished.
> [*Obsession.*]

Baudelaire, Platonist that he was, does not seem to have conceived the idea of omnipresent Christian eternity. His sempiternity is a gulf of existence, a *Karma*. His infinity is not the *abyssus infinitudinis* of the mystics; it is the *unknown* into which one precipitates himself, "insatiably avid for the dark and the uncertain" (*Horreur sympathique*). Since the fall is fatal, why this avidity? So as to escape the lure of the *avalanche,* the sensation of hyperconscious and leaden passivity, so atrociously familiar. A perpetual impatience about the future, symmetrical to a perpetual nostalgia: prophecy of memory, quest of future reminiscences, these aspects of the same *attention* which seeks to overflow the present existence in the two directions of duration give at least the illusion of *creating,* of giving rise to the new and of finding there again the eternal. The instinct to rejoin "the past life" to the term of the infinite fall is the force which deepens the gulf, a force that memory or memorial dream continually attracts. Perhaps, for lack of reintegration, this rememoration and the correspondences that it prefigures are the form of mystical ecstasy bound to the gulf, this latter being deepened to reach the former. However it may be, if the deepening of the abyss is ineluctable, the manner of deepening it can manifest a personal plan, within the limits of necessity. The *Epigraphe pour le livre condamné* requires this lucidity in the gulf itself, also of the reader. Placed under the invocation of Saturn, god of the Golden Age but also of Chaos, this "orgiastic and melancholy" book is suitable only for the reader who has conquered his vertigo as the author has triumphed over his: by a singular knowledge of the gulf, a laying bare of a remorse and an oblivion, all the way to their common source.

> Inquisitive soul that suffers
> And keeps on seeking paradise,
> Pity me! . . . or else, I curse you!

What is this knowledge of the gulf, this "hysteria" cultivated by Baudelaire "with joy and terror"? It arises from an abyssal pity at the spectacle of universal degradation. This pity does not turn away, neither does it act; it sees. The *sympathetic horror* is nothing more than an almost voluptuous mimesis before the suffering or vertigo of others; aesthetic participation, a kind of incomplete dividing where the detached spirit analyzes the *affects* that the psyche espouses; a manner of being both without and within, which corresponds to the ensemble of fatality for Baudelaire. "Glory is to remain *one* and to prostitute oneself in a particular fashion" (*J.I.,* 92). This sentence fixes the limits of a participation that Paul Arnold defined so well: "In sharing their joys and their pains, the poet neither hopes nor desires to diminish the burden of the sufferings of others. It is not a question of theological, Christian virtue; it is not a question of charity. The poet alone benefits from this transference. The hyperconsciousness is exercised in a more absolute and a more pure manner in the case of passions and virtues stirring the soul of a fellow man, that one lives or relives oneself in a mirage, like the actor." By the exercise of the only imaginative faculty, which preserves the specificity of beauty, all the passions can be experienced to the fullest without being in any way taken under control.

The most beautiful success of this technique is the poem *Delphine et Hippolyte,* evoking a frenzied Sapphic love. Under the guise of feminine homosexuality, all the themes dear to Baudelaire, difficult to handle in the form in which he saw them, are systematically aggravated to the end of their delirious logic. The *empty* act, imaginary, doubly sterile physically and mentally, gives to the unconsciousness the freedom to be swallowed up without risk. Nowhere else in *Les Fleurs du Mal* does the eloquence of the gulf attain such a degree of conviction: it is because here the movement of the passions is without resistance, the forbidden furiously explored through and through, then carried off in the infernal maelstrom. The love of two women, their emulation, triumphant or desperate, in the conquest of hell, is not only, like any love risks being, a counterreligion: it is counternature. By his transfer, the poet both neutral and possessed seizes the scope of the sacrilegious ambition that Delphine communicates to the "sister of [her] choice." A somber enthusiasm animates the poem, like "the raging wind of carnal desire," pure here of all blindness, assumed with the intensity of an inverse faith, and which the active partner calls love, the passive one hell. Their antinomy—no doubt the reason for their reciprocal "choice"—reveals two extremes of satanism. Love, in Delphine, is doubled with a will for a frantic uniquity; remorse, in Hippolyte, with a craving for annihilation no less great. Those are two opposite ways of destroying oneself and of killing one another, to wish for the fatal gulf together and, contradictorily, to turn away from the last horror of the gulf, deep down inside oneself. Once this horror is seen face to face, there is no longer a question of *making* one's destiny: one has only to submit to it.

A certain negative perfection can be attained in the consciousness of the *irremediable:* the rigor of a lucid, solitary fall, less and less troubled by the effort to escape it. It is this theme, in preference to any other, which seems to express the attitude peculiar to Baudelaire: the knowledge of the gulf ceases to be imaginary there and leads to a definite spiritual state. The descending spiral of the *irremediable* in the poem bearing this name is remarkably analyzed by Luzius Keller: as [the spiral] contracts, time solidifies and becomes empty. Hollowed out by the original fall, "far from the sight of God," of a spirit drawn by the evil form across three spiritual worlds superimposed, the gulf coils downward in accordance to the seven circles of hell, represented by the first seven stanzas. All the major symbols of Baudelaire are caught up in the implacable swirl. Let us single out that of the celestial spirit fallen into matter, which appears like a nightmare, the weight of an enormous *incubus*. One thinks of *La Cloche fêlée,* whose "striving desperately" to disengage itself from past deaths which crush it corresponds to the "groping futility" of the bewitched mind by the sempiternal recurrence of the eddies, that make a damned one of the angel that they suffocate; this obsessional imagery, which elsewhere, beginning with the opening *Au Lecteur,* displays our unconscious chaos, is constricted, concentrated, petrified by and against the consciousness which pierces it and whose perfect limpidity unifies it with its ultimate gangue of crystal.

"God does well what he does," says Garo concerning the order of things. In Baudelaire's judgment, this well-made order is that of the Devil, master of the material universe, while at the same time its permanent prisoner. The perfection of the demonic conscience coincides with its autoincarceration in its own self; the descent is the *emblem* of an interiorization with no way out, of a knowledge of the ultimate of depths. Saint Paul tells us that in the interior vision we reflect the glory of God as if in a mirror: here the creature fundamentally contemplates only the self. According to Isaac the Syrian, "The one who has seen his sin is greater than the one who has seen the angels." Here the creature deep within contemplates only Satan. This *within* "that no eye in Heaven can pierce," itself inverted Heaven where "a pale star shines," the star of death and damnation, the opposite of the *Stella matutina* of salvation, is a mirror enchanted by itself, a gulf gaping toward the top and toward the bottom and—who knows? —finally deprived of being like the smooth surface of a mirror. Immobile and alone in any case, the creature is reduced to the contemplation of his own void: fascinating-fascinated conscience, prisoner of itself like a beacon that has nothing to illuminate. This satanic light, this black fire, is pure Evil, without any determination: "consciousness in Evil," identified with matter in its principle, therefore liberated, relieved of all formal ascendancy and, by this fact, knowing itself to be in its somber spiritual glory forever rejected.

"Life has only one real charm: that is the charm of *Gaming*. But suppose we are indifferent to winning or losing?" (*J.I.,* 15). And how would the one who has, once and for all, reached the bottom, not be indifferent? To whoever feels in an absolute manner not that he himself, but that *his life* is damned from the beginning and forever, that his curse is for eternity the fact of living, of existence, offers literally no *gamble:* all is gulf, nothing distracts from the gaping tête-à-tête. But this "good news of the damnation" (Bloy) is intolerable; it is, as T. S. Eliot says, in vain that it is an immense relief and even "a form of salvation—of salvation from the tedium of modern life." This salvation is not in the faith, but in the bitter glory, the heroism of despair. For this latter, is not the most frightful temptation that of useless illusion?

> My heart took fright at its envy of so many
> Wretches running fiercely to the yawning chasm,
> Who, drunk with their own blood, would prefer, in a word,
> Suffering to death and hell to nothingness!
>
> [*Le Jeu.*]

It is true that opposite temptation is not less vain, although it seems to respond better, upon initial examination, as much to the incapacity for being, which is one of the dominant neuroses of Baudelaire, as to the immobility of the lucid conscience frozen in its damnation. "I wish to sleep! to sleep rather than live!" What more natural wish for the spirit knowing its life to be damned no matter what it does? Just as the poet envies "the stubborn passion" of gamblers, he is jealous of the sleep of animals, the unconscious, deceptive unity. If he cries out, in *Le Goût du Néant:* "Resign yourself, my heart; sleep your brutish sleep," this resignation is to despair what doubt is to faith. On the contrary, the highest degree of consciousness is fervor of the abyss for the "pious poet, enemy of sleep."

In fact, the risk of sleep is worse than that of games of chance. Sleep allows the powers from down below to penetrate the world above, to fabricate evil in sleeping, and thus to burden the mind with new determinations. Is that what Baudelaire fears, when he wishes to attain, by an indefatigable mental control, a state of desperate ataraxy? Certainly, he is "afraid of sleep as one is of a great hole"; he is no less attracted by this abyss which opens up at the bottom of his own abyss: *Abyssus abyssum invocat.* No doubt he shares the feeling of Joseph de Maistre: "Sleep is one of the great mysteries of man. The one who would understand it, would have, it appears, penetrated all the others." Even if the descending spiral of the fall is confused with the ascending stairway of dream, evoked at the beginning of *Tentations,* this alembic of evil spirits also distills visions of another order. Baudelaire distinguishes natural dream from *hieroglyphic* dream,[3] which "evidently represents the supernatural side of life, and it is precisely because it is absurd that the ancients thought it divine" (*P.A.,* 16). Such a dream as drugs can stimulate constitutes a "symbolic and moral tableau, engendered in the very mind of the man who sleeps. It is a dictionary that must be studied, a language to which the sages have lost the key." Is it engendered, or merely revealed, like a writing in invisible ink? Does it partake of our *incommensurable memory,* "divine palimpsest created by God" and put in order by "the fatality of temperament," which could be the unity of the spirit through its mysterious migration? This indestructible identity, although unknown in its essence, is contradictorily "consoling or terrible": "Just as all action, instigated in the vortex of universal action, is in itself irrevocable and irreparable, abstraction made of its possible results, so is every thought ineffaceable."

The search for identity through drugs or magic, while believing to economize on the descent into hell, results in a "frightful marriage of man with himself" (*P.A.*). For the poet of *Les Fleurs du Mal,* the orphic test seems inevitable, and requires a very strict lucidity. In view of what? Of the definitive tête-à-tête with the double, "latent Lucifer who is housed in every human heart": transcendent and immanent, gulf of an unfathomed fall, transparence of a spirit which is always watching. Vigilance at its peak at the moments of vast solipsism in which Baudelaire, in a space built with Pelagian architecture, lives, alone, the myth of the fallen man. This type of hieroglyphic dream, awake or not, is related to a fallen state; far from aspiring to recover it there, the dreamer goes deeply into his fall, the feeling of which is the only nobility of the damned. But the more this nobility is conscious, the more the suffering from it is infernal. What is one to seek then, hyperconsciousness or stupor? More and more as his neurosis grows worse, Baudelaire is assailed by the temptation of a state without images, veritably "beyond the possible, beyond the known." Temptation, and not aspiration, because he cannot prevent himself from condemning this desire immediately after having defined it: "To know nothing, to teach nothing, to want nothing, to feel nothing, to sleep, and sleep more, such is today my only wish. A base and disgusting wish, but sincere" (Proposal for a preface to a supplement for *F.M.*).

We could read in that a death wish, the final assault of the instinct of destruction which has not ceased gnawing at the poet who is careful to describe the progess of it. But death is only one episode of the fall: in *Le Rêve d'un curieux,* Baudelaire prepares himself to die, like the child to be born, to tear himself from the maternal womb; the end of the dream instructs him about the fact that after this birth beyond the tomb, sempiternal existence continues without death's having changed anything. Now the unknown is the only reason for desiring Death, the only motive of a hope which has nothing theological about it, being only a compensatory dream. When Baudelaire, before his unsuccessful attempt at suicide, wrote to Ancelle: "I am killing myself because I believe that I am immortal, and because I hope"[4] (June 30, 1845), the last verb is suspended, with no complement, and this hope is an empty wager. We are in the theater, waiting for, "hoping for," a second act better than the first, free, moreover, to leave the room, the only *act of hope* that Baudelaire conceives of. "What! You have never had the desire *to leave,* just to have a change of scenery! I have very serious reasons to pity the one who does not like Death" (to Jules Janin, *Œ.P.,* I, 230).

In Baudelaire's mythology, Death (with a capital letter) appears sometimes not like a passage, but like a *place.* "Have you then come to this degree of dullness that you are happy only in your evil? If such is the case, let us flee toward the countries which are the analogies of Death" (*N'importe où hors du monde, P.P.P.*). This dullness—one of the themes of *Les Fleurs du Mal*—rejection of the real and defense against it, we have seen that it is accompanied by a keen consciousness of the fall, which takes its pleasure at the point of its lucidity, in incurable nostalgia. Thus countries analogous to Death are paradisiacal dreams, projected before the dreamer who is attracted by the colors of definitive regret. In the bosom of life, the love of Death is perpetuated as form—atrophied, mutilated, but faithful—by the indestructible memory of which the gulf is the unfathomable echo. "The love of death has always reigned in me simultaneously with the love of life. I have enjoyed life with bitterness" (*Œ.P.,* III, 8). To love death is then to live in infinite nostalgia. Which does not prevent one from fearing the physical passage of death, this analogy with birth: "There is only one second in the human life which has the mission of announcing good news, *good news* which causes each one an inexplicable fear" (*La Chambre double, P.P.P.*).

In the last years of the poet the idea of death, however, becomes odious to him because, as he wrote to his mother, "it would reduce all my plans to nothingness, and because I have not yet carried out a third of what I have to do in this world" (letter of January 1, 1865). Sentiment of obligation linked no doubt to that of a ransom to pay, either to pass to another existence, or for a total remission of his debt. *La Rançon* like *L'Imprévu* announces a last Judgment, an end of times (a rare vision in Baudelaire), and a judge who in the first version is God, in the other Satan, demanding the price of his complaisances. This last poem, dedicated to Barbey d'Aurevilly, is of a Christian accent, cruel but indisputable; nowhere, except in *Bénédiction,* is there read such a certainty of the saving nature of suffering as the gift of God, as opposed to this sorrowful damnation in which the demon puts his glory. But these texts are the exception in *Les Fleurs du Mal,* whereas those abound which suggest a chrysalid existence after death. The feeling of the soul still attached to the physical remains, a past life and eventual transmigrations. Fog and rain often play the role of an uncertain frontier, of an osmotic element between the world of the living and that of the dead, spleen being the propitious humor in such an osmosis, manifested by an afflux of enigmatic memories. This same splenetic inspiration makes of the poet the medium of an indefinite number of past lives and perhaps of relative identities. Let us refer to the admirable definition that he gives to his "sad brain":

> It is a pyramid, a vast burial vault
> Which contains more corpses than potter's field.
> —I am a cemetery abhorred by the moon,
> In which long worms crawl like remorse
> And constantly harass my dearest dead.
>
> (*Spleen,* LXXVI.)

This evocation, and many other similar ones, could be compared to the exhausting quest of a way out that the dead make in *Le Repos du VII° jour* of Claudel:

> I hear in my soul a moaning sound
> As if from a multitude seeking, with this word: Ah! Ah!
> Ah! Ah! Where? Where?
> . . .
> In the never returning steps, in the vast and vain detour,
> In the day of the Night without night and without tomorrow,
> With this word: Ah! Ah! Where? Where? with horror and
>   terror we become confused in error,
> We search for
> The way and the issue, no end to the deluded hunger!

Death, such as Baudelaire sees it, is not the end: scarcely is it an accident of the fall. In the *post mortem* supernaturalism Baudelaire had for his master E. A. Poe. For the latter, as for Swedenborg, *anima* not annihilated by death lives a foetal existence, until the body is completely destroyed; then, completely liberated from it, *anima* becomes autonomous again. In Poe's *The Colloquy of Monos and Una*, "those admirable pages which would have charmed and troubled the flawless de Maistre," can be read an impressive description of the chrysalid existence during the years when the exterior covering disintegrates: "For *that* which *was not*, for that which had no form, for that which had no thought, for that which had no sentience, for that which was soulless, yet of which matter formed no portion—for all this nothingness, yet for all this immortality, the grave was still a home, and the corrosive hours, co-mates" (*N.H.E.,* 269). Thus Monos tells his Una the phases of a waiting which, by degrees of consciousness more and more attenuated, emerges on their common resurrection. For these two spirits, as their names indicate, are linked

together by an eternal election: an idea that Baudelaire effects
through the grievous reciprocity which unites him to Jeanne
Duval. This amorous correspondence, one would almost say this
reciprocal identity, is translated, in *La Mort des Amants,* by the
image of the "twin mirrors"; their death is the exchange of "a
single flash," ultimate and initial dialogue in the heart of the
One. But the serene vision of the hereafter is rare in the poet.
"The dead, ah! the poor dead suffer great pains," and sometimes
the worm gnaws them like a "posthumous remorse." The *ransom*
of eternity cannot be accomplished in a single *harvest;* several
barns must be filled. A sempiternal work perhaps, of which *Le
Squelette laboureur* offers us the lamentable spectacle, "emblem"
analogous to that of *L'Irrémédiable,* this fall from existence to
existence of which the demon is the toll-collector:

> Tell me, what singular harvest,
> Convicts torn from cemeteries,
> Do you reap, and of what farmer
> Do you have to fill the barn?

Now, Baudelaire is bound on earth to Jeanne Duval exactly
"like the convict to his chain"; their bond, in eternity, becomes "a
mystical, brotherly bond"; thus, "still more than Life, Death
holds us frequently with subtle bonds." Whether it is a question,
as it is here, of mutual election and vampirism, or elsewhere of
more general solidarity of destiny, life and death are interacting:
our world is full of "wandering spirits with no country" which
no doubt are seeking a body. Still more, the sempiternity—whose
image in the terrestrial mirror is boredom—is not entirely unconscious. "I am several centuries old already, since it seems to me
that I have worked, thought, at different epochs" (*Œ.P.,* III, 8-9).
The past lives are so many cadavers, sketchy identities, for which
the poet is the "common grave." Does this sempiternity have

integration as its end? If the poet sometimes suggests it, it is in a sufficiently ambiguous manner so that one reads in it either the growth of a future unity, or, through the effort of memory, the spectral outline of an anterior (or interior?) integrity which lasts forever.

> The forms disappeared and were no more than a dream,
> A sketch that slowly falls
> Upon the forgotten canvas, that the artist completes
> From memory alone.
>
> (*Une Charogne.*)

Degradation of the eternal in time, sempiternity is only one aspect of another degradation: that of form in matter. Time—that other name of remorse—is at work like essential sorrow, represented, in *Les Fleurs du Mal,* by all that gnaws, corrodes, teems, feeding on what it destroys. Sorrow and duration are synonyms for the unhappy conscience, which is its own inevitable mirror—its damnation perceived like time. In whatever manner he knows it, man knows that he lasts forever, that time engulfs him. "Tomorrow, after tomorrow, always!" such is the epitaph of this living death. But if matter is the degradation of form, it remains the enigma of it; the brain-cemetery of *Spleen* (LXXVI) is always the *sacred sanctuary* where, according to Swedenborg, the relations between man and infinity are pursued. We shall see how, in his moral of the dandy, Baudelaire illustrates the Gnostic idea: spiritual man is incorruptible. Whence the ambivalence of the gulf, which can also be a way: the original identity, lost in matter, is also *hidden* there. In placing *Bénédiction* at the beginning of *Les Fleurs du Mal,* in opposition to the preliminary *Au Lecteur,* Baudelaire, "the disinherited Child," placed himself in the double perspective of the "pilgrimage" and of the descent into hell. His "theory" of correspondences is not new, it is the *per speculum in aenigmate* common to all esoterism. In one sense, the world of exile is nothing more than the world of unity—of which, however, it is the inverse. The images of the cavern, tomb, vault, and sepulchre, matricial in Baudelaire, correspond to the Platonistic image of a here-below conceived like a "cosmic crypt" (Corbin), a place of genesis as much as reclusion. That, in his cavern, the "painter" in memories sees rise up "a specter made of grace and of splendor," the beloved in her eternal beauty, metaphor of total Reality, that suggests a possible opening to the "vault whose key is lost." Liberated from time and from expanse, eternity is *the same* which has become *something completely different:* in the cavern, it subsists then by *memory,* the only act which brings us in nostalgia close to the state of the Angel, which Swedenborg describes in this manner: "Although everything in heaven appears absolutely like it does on earth, in one place and in one space, the fact remains that the Angels have no notion whatsoever nor any idea of place and space." Inversely, we possess a certain power of recollection of the lost condition, or, says Swedenborg also, an interior memory, the guardian of memories not collected by the exterior memory.

Baudelaire gives a name to this interior memory: "the faculty of revery." Its place is the forest of symbols, the domain also of the *nevermore.*

> A whole far-away world, absent, almost defunct,
> Dwells in your depths, aromatic forest!
>
> (*La Chevelure.*)

Depths which constitute the part of the gulf, the spectralization of space and time. "Elsewhere, far, far from here! too late, *never* perhaps!" But by the law of ambivalence, the *forest where his spirit takes exile* is that where reverberates, multiform and one, the unfathomable evocation of the poet, like "a call from hunters

lost deep in the woods!" The theme of the mystical chase, all
the more poignant because, in it, it is the heart which aims at
the heart. That the poet is the accursed hunter, on trail of the
ineffable Being while at the same time tracked by it, that is his
ambiguity and his grandeur, his "neurosis" and his spiritual
perception. In his burning and very Chestovian exegesis of Baudelaire, Benjamin Fondane speaks familiarly of the depths, of the
neurotic or primitive thought which maintains, through nostalgia, certain great, fundamental rhythms. He shows also the mis-
trust of the philosopher before poetic activity, under which this
latter "has a foreboding of the living, eternal actuality of this
thought, repressed doubtlessly but not annihilated, capable of
living a crafty life, mutilated, disguised, sacrificed while awaiting
its hour." This thought is not motivated, as certain critics seem to
affirm, merely by the unconscious need to create, between desire
and its object, the mirage of distance: one could just as readily,
and in a way as little valid, reduce the *eternal distance* of the
mystics to the mirage of an infinite *self*. To call spirituality as J.
P. Richard does, "this ambiguous dimension, this distance—sometimes physical, sometimes interior—which separates Baudelaire
from things and from himself, but which at the same time
announce him and reunite him to himself and to the world," is to
pay little heed to the transcendent reality and the seriousness of
his lived experience. Moreover, on the psychological level, the
definition of J. P. Richard is no less mysterious (whether it
concerns Baudelaire or the poetic nature in general) than, for
example, the poetic operation described by Charles du Bos, according to which the artist conceives abstractions "all together
like archetypes toward which, without hope of ever being
able to proceed wholly to the source, always it is necessary to hold
out, and like receptacles, vases of plenitude of which, once obtained, a few drops would suffice for the most ambitious transmutations." If it is true that "each man carries within him his dose of

natural opium, incessantly secreted and renewed" (*L'Invitation au Voyage, P.P.P.*), it is also true, for the same Baudelaire, that to return "in the real way of poets" is to obey "the ineluctable truth which haunts us like a demon." (The demon, here as for Socrates, is the familiar spirit, the part of the divine which resides in us.)

Certainly we ask ourselves how this "ambiguous dimension," so well studied by J. P. Richard, *can* be religious, in what way it is not so or deviates sacrilegiously. But we shall begin with the idea that the religious experience is neither an aesthetic fabrication nor a self-creative process immanent to the one who enjoys it, and so also with the conviction that one and the other can always fake this experience, adulterate it, indeed, substitute the self for it. When Baudelaire cries out with this *love of art* in which he puts his nobility: "Poetry is what there is that is most real, it is what is completely true only in *another world*" (*Œ.P.*, 299), or when he praises Fromentin for possessing "a faculty which is not feminine," that of "seizing parcels of beauty scattered out over the earth, for following beauty's trail everywhere that he could slip through the trivalities of fallen nature" (*C.E.*, 318), he does not give himself the transcendence of beauty as an element of his poetic machinery; he feels it, it enters into his *religion*. Memory is the mystical form of this religion: the substance that it seizes is beauty. For the man "consumed by a love of beauty," life is a tomb, a hell, where he preserves, by the increasing suffering of exile, the innate experience of his true nature. Experience which, from out of the unconscious depths, springs up in this world in the form of poetry. In Baudelaire's aesthetic itself, a metaphysic is incorporated. The *short* poem, fruit of a slow crystalization of time in eternity, is a moment of Unity, a victory of every being against multiplicity. What bursts forth in images is the enigmatic memory of an identity which englobes our apparent one: it is the blood of the *Wholly One,* of the Center, of the Heart. This divine Heart, E. A. Poe reminds us, *"is our own heart."* And he adds this, which can so well be applied to Baudelaire, and according to which the feeling of eternity would be the coenesthesia of the eternal person in us:

> We walk about, amid the destinies of our world-existence, encompassed by dim but ever present *Memories* of a Destiny more vast—very distant in the bygone time, and infinitely awful. We live out a Youth peculiarly haunted by such shadows; yet never mistaking them for dreams. As Memories we *know* them (*Eureka*).

In Baudelaire, this impregnation by memory does nothing except bring us back, beyond "the deep years," to the enigma of an incommensurable destiny. The word memory (*souvenir*), so frequently used by the poet, must be understood in its etymologi cal freshness, in the manner that Theodor Haecker stresses when he writes in his *Métaphysique du sentiment:* "Spiritually and dynamically, it designates the way that leads to the Spirit through the interior; that is to say, the road that leads to the invisible, or at any rate to the frontier of the visible and the invisible, to the point where thought and image, like also thought and action, make only one and are mingled, this frontier which separates the perceptible from pure spirit." It is difficult to state precisely if Baudelaire, independently of memories acquired through existence, has the conception of Memory of an anterior-interior Life for every existence: or else if the memories accumulated through the successive lives are so many indications of a nostalgic, indefinite return toward a Reality outside all memory. He does believe on the one hand, judging from *Le Flacon,* that the memory of a past existence can serve as a lure in view of inducing the soul to be born again; on the other, that in the elective relation binding two spirits together, each one is the indestructible memorial of the other. *Le Flacon* furnishes the proof that Baudelaire's spiritualism is a materialism and inversely; matter being a degradation of the spirit, not only does it retain the traces of it, but this latter, in breaking down, becomes fluid in order to penetrate it: sounds, perfumes, colors, partake of essence. Matter is then saturated with spirit, truly peopled with spirits. Deep within things, which are apparently inanimate, dramas are acted out in the invisible.

> Sometimes one finds an antique phial which remembers,
> Whence gushes forth a living soul returned to life.

This return liberates from their "death-like chrysalids" thoughts which are attracted to each other and gather together in memory and in vertigo. Two specters are now met, clutching at each other, throwing each other down "at the edge of an ancient abyss," that of the sempiternal fall back into which they cast each other in resuscitating. Reincarnated, reincarcerated in matter one by the other, they remain united by the same eternal bond. Each one, no matter what the degradation that it still undergoes, as "desolate, decrepit, dusty, dirty, abject, slimy, cracked" as it can become, remains evocative of the other, whom it keeps in memory like an eternal balm for the essentially anterior splendor "behind the tomb" which is every life. It is thus that in her "spiritual flesh," distillation of the matter in which she is enclosed, woman becomes again for Baudelaire a "Being, lucid and pure," shadow and memory of inaccessible Reality.

Love is indeed, with the poet, at the same time a call of the abyss and an aspiration toward supreme Reality: it is the ideal of Sodom and of the Virgin Mother, interdependent because they are contradictory. At their common source, the childhood situation reappears. Contradictory, unattainable, love sharpens remorse and solitude, the true propulsive force behind Baudelairian religiosity, drawn, not without complaisance, between an eternally lost beatitude, and a sempiternal malediction. "What a tête-à-tête a corrupt heart using itself as a mirror would have" (letter to Poulet-Malassis). Still it is permitted to think of this heart "peaceful as a sage and gentle as an accursed one," thus in ecstasy in the irremediable, either consumed by a love in the hollow of the absolute of which the nostalgia of the womb would be the open wound, the real figure; and the impotence to love, the negative. In *The Book of Ecstasy* of ibn al A'rabi, one reads concerning certain raptures: "Each time that they see a mirage, they believe that it is a spring of water, and each time they see a spring of water, they believe it is a mirage, precisely because of this avidity which has dominated them. They go through life without paying attention to anything, wandering through each valley, pursuing each cloud at the center of which appears a flash of lightning. It is water without rain, these are memories without ideas . . . They resemble most the insane, for their souls have generously allowed the ruination of their lives in the pursuit of their goals." And the Moslem poet adds: "They benefit from no advantage, except that of being protected from turpitude by their fidelity."

2. *The Dandy Lucifer*

Baudelaire's life is a continual fall from grace, in contrast to an indefatigable lucidity. From one step to another, along that fall, one sees his destiny solidify, become immobile. The upward cry is only the more imperious in its tragic affirmation. In short, the poet's existence is the first of his symbols, from which the others are derived, and which they accentuate. This symbol moves in two opposite but indissociable directions: fall and elevation. If the fall, for Baudelaire, has not become his very essence, it is because of the consciousness of his fallen grandeur: consciousness which, dialectically, is also the sense of the fall. "The angelic element and the diabolic element function in a parallel manner" (*De l'Essence du Rire, C.E.,* 381). If sometimes the malicious force seems to stimulate *a contrario* another force oriented toward good, most often, the consciousness is incapable of any good and is only whetted against its own self. Fallen, man cannot help seeing the separation become aggravated. In consciously confirming its enslavement, the spirit goes deeply into its nostalgia for the heights from which it has fallen; this vigilance in memory is the only elevation permitted by evil—one would almost have to say thanks to evil.

The theme of the two postulations rationalizes this ambivalence.

> There are in every man, at every moment, two simultaneous postulations, one toward God, the other toward Satan. The invocation to God, or spirituality, is a desire to rise in dignity; that of Satan, or animality, is a joy of descending (*J.I.,* 62).

A well-known principle, which Baudelaire did not entirely invent, since one finds it in Swedenborg stated like this: "Man is submitted to two opposite influences, emanating, one from God, the other from the Prince of this world, one from the love of supreme Good, the other from the love of the greatest evil." The idea of these forces is no less explicit in Joseph de Maistre: "The more one examines the universe, the more one feels inclined to believe that evil comes from a certain division that one does not know how to explain, and that the return to good depends on a contrary force which drives us unceasingly toward a certain unity just as inconceivable." According to Swedenborg, *animus,* the external, inferior man, and *anima,* the inner man, unalterable, struggle with each other in the mind of every human being, by the intermediary, the one of malicious spirits, the sensual passions, the other of celestial *amores,* the ideal conceptions. Baudelaire takes up for his own use this personification of evil intelligences, which constitute the sinister vermin and the monstrous fauna of *Les Fleurs du Mal.* Like Swedenborg and many others, he depicts his Guardian Angel under the traits of a real woman:

but whereas the Swedish visionary assigns a celestial role to physical love, the poet sees in it most often an exercise of the damnation; the flesh is for him "the diabolical part of man." However, it happens that man may be "gratified" by a "beatitude," "after culpable orgies of the imagination" like those that hashish brings on; but this "grace" is in fact "a recall to order under a complementary form" (*P.A.,* 5). Baudelaire could say, like Dimitri Karamazov: "Extremes touch each other, contradictions live joined together [. . . .] It is the duel of the devil and God, the human heart being the battle field."

One of the most beautiful pages that Baudelaire has devoted to this struggle—and to the passion upon which it feeds—is his commentary on *Tannhaüser.* In Richard Wagner's masterpiece, after a furious mêlée in which the demon has the upper hand for a long time, God triumphs; here is how this great duel is described:

The *Pilgrims' Chorus* appears first, with the authority of the supreme law, as though to mark at the outset the true direction of life, the goal of the universal pilgrimage, which is God. But as the intimate sense of God is soon drowned in every consciousness by the lusts of the flesh, the motif which represents holiness is gradually overwhelmed by the sighs of the senses. The true, terrible and universal Venus is already looming up in every imagination [. . . .] Languors, fevered and agonized delights, ceaseless returns towards an ecstasy of pleasure which promises to quench, but never does quench, thirst; frenzied palpitations of heart and senses, imperious orders of the flesh, the whole onomatopoeic dictionary of Love is to be heard here. Finally the religious theme little by little resumes its sway, slowly, by degrees, overwhelming the other at last in a peaceful victory, as glorious as that of the irresistible being over his sickly and anarchic adversary, of St. Michael over Lucifer (*A.R.,* 221).

To write such a text, the poet must have recognized his own inner war in the creatures of the musician; and even, under the

magic effect of art, he could believe the Wagnerian resolution of
the conflict between the postulations not only desirable but possible. But his work, taken as a whole, refutes this hope of a final
triumph. All happens as if the duel were only an appearance, the
representation of a debate without end that the conscience carries
on with itself. In this perspective, one can compare *L'Avertisseur*
to *La Voix*, published at the same period. This latter poem is in
the singular although two voices are addressing the child: he
answers in the familiar form of address only to the second voice,
which calls him "beyond the known." Or perhaps he joins them
in a single ambiguous reality, the cause of his *wound* and of his
fatality. Is this double voice the warning, the host lodged in the
heart, in the center-abyss of "every man worthy of this name,"
therefore conscious in Baudelaire's fashion? Is the resolution of
the conflict in advance, with no hope of an alternative, in this
consciousness of evil, "permanent principle of separation" (Cré-
pet-Blin), which constantly reminds man of that of the postulations provoking his present desire? Are "Ormuz and Arimane"
the same, as Cramer shouts?

A question which comes back to this last: Is the interdict the
mask of essence? All Baudelaire is in the antinomic identification
of the secret and of the forbidden. "The dolorous secret" of *La
Vie Antérieure* is anterior to every imaginable existence. In
Spleen the secrets of the brain are those of an immense cemetery.
"Living is an evil. That's a secret known to all" (*Semper eadem*).
The noise which escapes, incongruous, from the "sweet and
amiable woman" of *Confession,* is the complaint of a part of
herself, repressed, "hidden . . . in a secret cellar." We have seen
that this cellar is the world, existence, the body: the echoes still
reach there from "a deep and tenebrous unity." *L'Invitation au
voyage,* "anywhere out of the world,"[5] contains the hope that

All would whisper there
Secretly to the soul
In its soft, native language.

This invitation is that hope to a woman: because the secret is of
an erotic nature, woman is down here the receptacle or the representation of it, this latter sometimes sacrilegious and all the more
seductive. Everything in her partakes of "that nature, strange and
symbolic," even to the "secret eye" of the garter on the leg of the
decapitated woman, the martyr. Temple of the secret, object of a
secret cult of a satanic character, the feminine flesh is a ritual
theater where aspiration toward the secret and vertigo brought
on by the forbidden sometimes oppose each other, sometimes
become mingled. A confrontation which amplifies, on another
symbolic level, the combat between *man and the sea,* "both . . .
gloomy and reticent," unfathomed, spiritually identical. Here the
secret and the forbidden are the two *deep appearances* of an
imperceptible reality that their depth represents in an incised
form. "For innumerable centuries this reality has been in a
struggle against itself, and man has been trying to penetrate his
own essence, through matter, absolute obstacle and unique way.
Fatal struggle, physical as well as spiritual, escaping from the
conventions of morality and from the limitations of value: the
real fighter is the abyss invoking the abyss, the only worthy
adversary.

The inner sense of the abyss is *remorse,* permanent verification
of the irremediable and the irreparable, and of the sempiternity
of the fall. It is the Eumenides, the eternal Vengeance: contrary
to repentance, remorse excludes pardon. Who takes revenge?
Who suffers the vengeance? The origin of the fall being
impenetrable, Baudelaire was able to conjecture that the creation
was the fall of God. Antinomy as old as the mind of man;

Berdyaev recalls, in *Le Sens de la Création,* that "for the greatest of the mystics, Jacob Boehme, evil was in God, and evil was the fall outside of God; the obscure source of evil was in God, and God, moreover, was not responsible for evil." If, in the poems comprising *Révolte,* Baudelaire rises up against God's justice, it is not to put in doubt, no matter how obscure the nature of it is, man's guilt. He admits, following Joseph de Maistre, that "man is guilty through his *principle* of *sensibility,* his flesh, his life." Moreover, he seems to believe, like Pascal (with whom, even if he hardly frequented him, he displays some common points studied by Maurice Chapelan), that "God would be unjust, if we were not guilty." With a logic which scandalized Rémy de Gourmont, "this man, whom the magistrates condemned like a monster of impiety and lewdness, knelt down very sincerely, after a fine bit of debauchery, to ask for pardon, and he accepted the punishment." The punishment, yes: but was he expecting redemption? He believes in "the operation of a vengeful mystery" of which certain *consecrated* beings are the instruments and the victims,

> When Vengeance beats out his hellish call to arms,
> And makes himself the captain of our faculties.
> [*Réversibilite.*]

Not only does vengeance pounce upon them as if on a prey, but, like a frightful inspiration, like an inverse Paraclete, it takes possession of their minds. Whence its ambiguity, which is evidently integrated with the deep-seated ambivalence attributed by Baudelaire to this type of men, scapegoats, sacred creatures. One could say, by emphasizing the extremes, that grief from remorse is God's vengeance, and that pride from remorse is man's vengeance. If it is true, as Fondane says, that "the problem of regret is given only to the disinherited, the only ones who admit nostalgia

for paradise," it is not less so that this nostalgia can be manifested
in a refusal, that of "the martyrs of an evil road" (*L'Irréparable*)
who have the pride of their "martyrdom."

Paul Arnold believes that Baudelaire "opposes to the need of
rehabilitation this terrible postulate that no action can repair the
perversion introduced by the transgression." Remorse would be
an implacable attention to an objective fact, the indestructible
memory of the evil inherent in the whole creation: in a word,
this would be the sacred character of the damned, which would
have the vocation of maintaining it, as if it were its vestal. Many
a passage in the work could serve to corroborate this thesis, were
it only this sentence, suspended, like a confession of the poet to
himself, from a letter to Madame Aupick: "I am so frightfully
unhappy that if I agree to go on living, it is for a deep reason that
you do not know!" (letter of July 4, 1859). Joseph de Maistre,
whose influence on Baudelaire can be seen on almost every page,
cites strangely, a short time after Leibniz's statement: "Every
wicked man is a self-torturer," a passage from the *Aeneid* which
can be rigorously applied to Baudelaire's theme, but especially to
the nature of his life: "Surrounding the wicked I always seem to
see the whole hell of poets, TERRIBLES VISU FORMAE [Figures
terrible to behold]: *voracious concerns, pale maladies, ignoble
and precocious old age, fear, indigence (the sad counsellor),
false joys of the mind, intestinal war, the vengeful furies,
black melancholy, sleep of the conscience and of death."* That is
indeed what the poet takes upon himself in becoming the *scapegoat* (letter to Arsène Houssaye, Christmas 1861). But at the
same time he fortifies this consciousness in evil from which he
draws indifferently a joy of honor or a contrary joy, like Stavro-
gin, his Dostoevskian brother. "It was not crime that I loved
(my intelligence in this case did not deceive me), but this joy that
the sorrowful consciousness of my deep baseness gave me," said
this latter in his *Confession*. Analyzing the satanic effects of the

drug, according to Thomas De Quincey, Baudelaire goes further than Dostoevski, to the point of showing how remorse kindles *enthusiasm* in the heart. Completing De Quincey by a direct observation, his analysis is that of an inspired precursor who ventures quite consciously to the limits of alienation.

> Remorse, the singular ingredient of pleasure, is soon drowned in the delicious contemplation of remorse, in a kind of voluptuous analysis; and this analysis is so rapid, that man, this natural devil, to talk like the Swedenborgians, does not perceive how it is involuntary, and how, from second to second, he comes close to diabolical perfection. He *admires* his remorse and he glorifies himself, while he is in the process of losing his liberty. There then is my hypothetical man, the spirit of my choice, arrived at this degree of joy and freedom where he is forced into self-admiration (*P.A.,* 58).

Such is one of the aspects of the *man-god* that Baudelaire, horrified and fascinated, contemplates in his own makeup.

But the other pole of consciousness in evil is the inveterate disgust with the self: it bursts forth, repeatedly, in the poet's correspondence. And not only with himself, but with man: "Has such a horror as man ever existed except in me?" (*Œ.P.*) In a rhetorical manner, that is to declare an absolute ambition. Ambition that *Les Fleurs du Mal* attests to also: "I do not feel at all guilty," wrote the poet, on the day of his condemnation, to the minister of state, Achille Fould. "I am on the contrary very proud of having produced a book which breathes only the terror and the horror of evil" (letter of July 20, 1857). For the exercise of the conscience, such as Baudelaire conceives it, objectifies evil and makes one capable of committing it without being the accomplice of it, since evil is the law of nature and of life. *To do evil knowingly,* motto of Baudelaire, is consciously to push evil to the extreme so that, reciprocally, it pushes consciousness to the absolute.

Alas! the vices of men, so full of horror as one supposes them to be, contain the proof (when it would be only their infinite expansion!) of his taste for the infinite; only, it is a taste that often mistakes its way [. . .] All leads to reward or punishment, two forms of eternity [. . .] It is in this deprivation of the sense of the infinite that lies, according to me, the reason for all culpable excesses. . . (*P.A.*, 6).

A text that sounds a conventionally Christian tone in its allusion to eternal rewards—an allusion that the final visions of *L'Imprévu* and of *Bénédiction* corroborate. But to be conscious in evil is to situate oneself, in an absolute manner, outside all hope for recompense, because beyond all possible effort one knows himself to be capable only of evil: "I am guilty toward myself;— this disproportion between the will and the faculty is for me something unintelligible. Why, having so just, so clear an idea of duty and utility, do I always do the contrary?" (letter to his mother, Mar. 26, 1853). The only salvation for such a conscience is in "the taste of the infinite" as such, to the point of greeting this taste in its worst depravity, without participating in it otherwise than through the attention given to the spectacle. The first to understand this was Barbey d'Aurevilly, who wrote: "The author of *Les Fleurs du Mal* has made himself villainous, blasphemous, impious through thought . . . He has performed a play, but it is the tragic play that Pascal talks about."[6] Positive evil in Baudelaire's life is very far from being in proportion to his consciousness, his suffering, in evil. The suffering and consciousness—for they are identical—present a frantic tension that his constantly intensifying reiteration forces us to see as the "raison d'être" of Baudelaire as poet and man, the absolute that, by its tautening, endlessly vivifies his spirit. Then we shall hear, in their tragic depth, ferocious complaints like these:

I am not a dupe, I have never been a dupe! I say *Long live Revolution!* as I would say *Long live Destruction! Long live*

Expiation! Long live punishment! Long live Death! Not only would I be happy to be the victim, but I would not hate being the executioner—to experience the Revolution in both manners. (*Pauvre Belgique! Œ.P.,* III, 216).

When he dreams of carousing with the crowd—as he did during the Days of February[7]—it is certainly not in order to participate in the "great social festivity," the nostalgia for which Sartre projects forward. If Baudelaire participated, it was probably in order to destroy. Like Sartre—who knows? Both believe in energy, but the names they give it differ: one calls it degradation, the other progress. This latter is not only for Baudelaire the "great heresy of decrepitude"; it is the sempiternal effrontery of bad faith. For him who, without ceasing to be lucid, wishes to be present at the irremediable fall and to verify absolute character, the progressive mentality is worse than stupid; it is diabolical because it is ingenuous. Therefore he does not have enough sarcasm for those having this mentality, from the Belgian free thinkers to George Sand, this *big animal* that the Devil has persuaded "to trust *her good heart* and *her common sense,* so that she might persuade all the other *big animals* to trust their good hearts and their common sense" (*J.I.,* 69). For, according to Baudelaire, faith in progress is definitive blindness, the substitution of general unconsciousness in well-being for personal consciousness in evil. "I mean by progress the progressive diminution of the soul and the progressive domination of matter (*C.E.,* 1859 version, 267). Moreover, an all the more frightful dupery, since it is "a conquest lost at each minute, a progress always negating itself" (*N.H.E.*). In the conquering fatality of progress, Baudelaire sees then a new stage in the fall, the identity of uncontrollable acceleration and ultimate solidification.

I put aside the question of knowing if, continually refining humanity in proportion to the new pleasures that it offers, indefinite progress would not be its most ingenious and its most cruel torture; if, proceeding by an obstinate negation of itself, it would not be a form of suicide forever renewed; and if, closed up within the fiery circle of divine logic, it would not resemble a scorpion which stings itself with its terrible tail, this eternal *desideratum* which makes its own eternal despair (*C.E.,* 228).

In writing that, Baudelaire, moreover, only takes back up—without realizing it?—a constant theme of the Tradition, given prominence again in our time by René Guénon in his criticism of the notion of progress: "That is what appears to us completely in an opposite fashion like a deep fall, for these are manifestly only the effects of the movement of fall, endlessly accelerated, which drags humanity down towards the 'lower depths' where the pure quantity prevails" (*Le Règne de la Quantité*).

Resolute adversary of the idea of a universal, exterior and mechanical progress, Baudelaire does not entirely dismiss that of an individual and inner progress. "In order that the law of progress exist, it would be necessary that each one should wish to create it; that is to say that when all the individuals will apply themselves to progressing, then, and only then, humanity will be in progress" (*J.I.,* 103). Must we, like Rolland de Renéville, see in this statement the influence of Wronski? This creation of interior humanity by the conjunctive effort of all its individuals is here only an hypothesis: the difference of tenses—from the subjunctive to the future—between the two parts of the aphorism gives it a dubitative tone. To read the reflection that follows this statement, one would say that this latter is in fact only the pretext of the former. "This hypothesis can serve to explain the identity of two contradictory ideas, freedom and fatality.—Not only will there be, in the case of progress, identity between freedom and fatality, but this identity is *history,* the history of nations and of individuals" (*J.I.,* 103). But the identity between freedom and fatality, is it not consciousness in evil, the only true inner "progress," the only one which escapes temporality? This identity has always existed, because there have always been *consecrated* natures, men *of* destiny and men *of the* destiny; this latter being a spiritual integral, *history,* conceived not as pure chronology, but as meta-temporal unity in Time even ideal and real at the same time. More than from Wronski, this manner of thinking comes from Joseph de Maistre. It takes a sharp turn in Baudelaire, who does not have the metaphysical head of the latter. Let us retain clearly what he is searching for in it: an image of freedom in fatality that he can make his own.

Is this identity realized in the dandy, of whom Baudelaire saw a model in de Maistre? "Before all else, to be *a great man* and *a saint* for one's self," such is the maxim of the Baudelairian ethic, and of the dandyism such as the poet recreates it. For it is indeed a question of a creation *ex nihilo,* and one not so far removed from the ambition that Wronski assigns to man to create himself in a way by fixing for himself his own end. The operation, it is true, is limited here only to the person of Baudelaire, for whom man in general, humanity, is only matter into which the fall precipitates him. *"Self-purification and antihumanity,"*[8] the for-mula has a false English air which, citation or not, symbolizes the egotistical will. This man wishes to owe himself only to himself, to hold values from no collectivity, were it even an ideal one. Let us recall a text that has already been cited: "An ideal is the indi-vidual rectified by the individual, reconstructed and restored [. . .] to the dazzling truth of his native harmony." The para-disiacal intention is then clearly affirmed: would it be a question, not of a reintegration by reminiscence only, but of hope for a real salvation? It must not be forgotten that "the dandy must live and sleep before a mirror," and that this "sombre and limpid tête-à-tête" defines the strict limits of his "salvation." Dandyism is an-other form of consciousness in evil, its sublimation in heroism and saintliness "for one's self." In this manner fatality and liberty become mingled; at the heart of the irreversible fall, one can be every day "the greatest of men." Even more: the victim and the sacrificer of a cult that one renders only to his own lucidity, immaculate and sorrowful under the whip of evil which punishes and the injury of evil which sullies.

> Strange spiritualism. For those who are at once the priests and the victims of it, all the complicated material conditions to which they submit, from the irreproachable toilette at every moment of the day and the night to the most dangerous feats of sport, are only gymnastics suitable to fortify the will and discipline the soul. In truth, I was not wrong in considering dandyism as a kind of religion (*A.R.*, 90).

Certainly; but let us not go so far as Stanislas Fumet, who sees in the spiritualism of the dandy "the antechamber of Christianity." Dandyism appears to us, as Baudelaire himself expressly defined it, like a self-idolatry, in the highest sense no doubt; for the poet —Charles du Bos expresses it well—"feels himself living only at the summit"; he seeks a sublimity "without interruption," but it is "before a mirror." Whence this equivocal mixture of asceticism and petty meticulosity, a spiritual aspiration which is sometimes reduced to a maniacal ritual, without control, but equally without recourse, a divided look which does not leave itself. We are still far from the prayer of the last years which consumes the dandy's ambition in imploring God to perfect it: "Give me the strength to do immediately my duty every day and to become thus a hero and a saint" (*J.I.*, 80). But there even, transmuted dandyism remains a *duty* that one sets for one's self. It is a prayer with a completely different accent which would ask God for the grace to do *his Will*.

The perfect dandy (Baudelaire lets it be understood in the definition that he lovingly formulates of his *Beauty*) is in short Satan—Milton's Satan, and his own. Georges Blin, so perspicacious in his analysis of Baudelaire's appetite for strength, of his nostalgia—and his jealousy—of "the sufficient life," notes accurately that "it is his need for eminence that he adores under the name of Satan." In the minor Romantics, satanism is fashionable: the great figure of Melmoth, creation of the Reverend Maturin, haunts equally Balzac and Baudelaire. "Let us remember Melmoth, this admirable emblem. His frightful suffering lies in the disproportion between his wonderful faculties, acquired instantly by a satanic act, and the milieu where, like a creature of God, he is condemned to live" (*P.A.,* 64). What is this satanic act? The usurpation—represented here by magic, but which can be achieved by drugs or by the consciousness exercised to its full capacity—of the powers and of the very nature of God: definition which is also applicable to the fall. Satan, "God betrayed by fate," is the twin brother of the other, the Cain of this Abel. According to the *Litanies* that Baudelaire devotes to him in the manner of many a poet of the period, Satan has at his disposal a secret apparently lost, buried in matter. Alone, those who share his exile invoke him as master of this secret, "accursed pariahs" to whom he teaches "through love the taste of Paradise," the irremediably nostalgic Vision, out of which is born, as in Tannhaüser, before the absolute of his crime, "the feeling almost ineffable, so terrible it is, of joy in damnation" (*A.R.,* 226). It is not arbitrary to see in *Les Litanies de Satan* an example of this "travestied religion" about which the poet claims: Satan is the damned one in his perfect resemblance to God; or alternately, the image of God in the spirit totally deprived of God. A god without God, and who in his damnation wishes to create himself the equal of this latter, while at the same time experiencing at every moment, in the effort to exceed himself constantly, his inability ever to do so.

The Satan of *Les Litanies,* whom Baudelaire invokes in this response:

O Satan, take pity on my long misery!

is no other than "Hermes the unknown" of *Alchimie de la Douleur.* If the fall is the alembic of nostalgia, this poem is the alchemical recipe for it.

> You have always frightened me,
> Hermes the unknown, you who help me.
> You make me the peer of Midas,
> The saddest of all alchemists;
>
> Through you I change gold to iron
> And make of paradise a hell;
> *(Alchimie de la Douleur.)*

Such is the satanic fashion of sympathizing with this "long misery" that the incurable sorrow of exile is. The demoniacal pity turns divine love aside, intimidates hope, assists the damned by fortifying him in his despair: remorse substituted for repentance makes the transgression *absolute.* Inversely, the idea of personal adhesion to salvation is repressed for the benefit of the fatality of the fall. The same force which represses, which "intimidates," "assists" in the creation of an irreversible equilibrium, excluding the repressed substance and faculty. Considering Baudelaire's life in its proper fatality, what can one think except that this redemptive substance is love, this faculty the capacity to love? Their absence will be compensated for by a capacity *to delve into it* to the point of making of love the eternal gulf of existence. Satan is not the "great king of subterranean things" for no reason, and images of concavity, numerous in *Les Fleurs du Mal,* are all of an "infernal" nature—desperate quest for the anterior life, in both directions of a sempiternity still to be lived or already lived.

It is permissible to recognize, in this desperate eagerness to deepen absolute deprivation endlessly, the negative of an absolute desire. Many commentators point out moreover that, at the period when the poet lived, only the demonic mask permitted spiritual dissatisfaction to accede to its subterranean world. Baudelaire himself saw clearly what views of the abyss were opened to the conscience of his time. Departing from Maturin, Byron, and Poe, who revealed the "latent Lucifer" in the heart of every man, he comes to the "essentially demonic tendency" of contemporary art. "It seems that this infernal part of man, that man delights in explaining to himself, increases daily, as if the Devil were amusing himself in fattening it through artificial means, like farmers, patiently stuffing the human species in his poultry-yards to prepare himself a more succulent food" (*A.R.*, 359). Let us observe with him, once more, the bitter vampirism of remorse, this "infernal part of man": the Devil, who "always does well what he does," constantly augments consciousness in evil, by means of his food. But man delights in explaining to himself this hell which opens up in his heart, therefore adding fuel to it within himself. Satan is not exterior to man, that is the law of his fall, personified. Fall and damnation are synonyms in Baudelaire's mind, bound up together with remorse for the loss, with the anterior absolute. A psychic cycle definitively closed to all recourse, this distillation of the consciousness is perhaps only the operation of a superior narcissism which evokes, in the person of Satan, the "mysterious being whom I had always desired to know and whom I recognized immediately, although I had never seen him" (*Le Joueur généreux, P.P.P.*). This Satan completely interiorized is in no way contradictory to the exterior *wicked force* whose *hypothesis* Baudelaire supports in a letter to Gustave Flaubert (June 26, 1860). If the evil thoughts of man can cause demons to blossom forth into a material existence, man can very easily be assailed from the exterior by a force which is nonetheless born from him.

A fine page from Paul Arnold, identifying the "Satan, Trismegist" of the poem *Au Lecteur* with "Hermes the unknown," reminds us that this Hermes, for the Alexandrians, is *"logos personified,* an attribute not *independent of the Creator."* He concludes that, for Baudelaire, Satan represents "the active, creative will of the Being, the knowledge of the formal, the finite, the real": that is to say, God in his fall. The satanic tendency is then "the desire to seek the formal world." In our turn, let us note that Hermes, the Thoth of the Egyptians, stole, *on the very day of his birth,* the flocks of his brother, Apollo. Later, he drove Cronos to mutilate his father, Uranos. Hermes-Thoth, inventor of the alphabet, master of the ambiguous word, is the magician who draws out of nothingness all that exists. Judge of the Dead, companion of souls—those that he steals from Apollo—he guides them to Hades and keeps the book of human deeds. Trismegist, Thrice-Great, he is, in his manifestations, the antithesis of God the trinitarian. Besides an original rhyme, his name furnished the poet a differently concentrated symbol than the trinitarian fantasy on man, the wine, and the Holy Spirit that can be found in the *Paradis Artificiels.* This anti-God is totally inscribed in the world that he creates himself, here below and in hell. He is the god of time sempiternal, the sphinx of an unfathomed secret, the preserver of irreparable acts. He is also the spirit of darkness, the anti-sun who, in being born, took the souls from Apollo. No doubt his magical power, beginning with nothingness, comes to him from this original infraction. This same Hermes, god of the double meaning, is sublimated like the Erinyes. Along winding paths, he leads toward a divine goal: he is called Sôter, Savior; from darkness, he becomes light. Did Baudelaire analyze and compare the various aspects of the myth of Hermes? Probably not; but a myth of this enigmatic quality constitutes a deep psychic aggregate, the elements of which are corresponding and interdependent. It is legitimate to suppose that the myth was selected unconsciously by the poet because the image of Hermes expressed a certain order of archaic tendencies for which Baudelaire, by his genial fatality, became an exceptional spokesman.

No approximation could seize the richness of the Baudelairian Satan. In simplifying, one can see in it not a fallen God, but the spirit considered as demiurge of its fall—the *natural Devil* of the Swedenborgians. About Melmoth, one of the great satanic representations of man, Max Milner could write: "the man-Melmoth disappears to give way to this supernatural being which unites, like a kind of infernal Christ, the two demonic and human natures." If it is true that "the sage par excellence, the Word incarnate, has never laughed" (*Ess. Rire,* in *C.E.,* 372), and that "in the viewpoint of the definitive absolute, there is no longer anything except joy," this laugh of Melmoth, this satanic attribute par excellence, is the abyss of his contradictory nature which is rent in order that he may be swallowed up.

> Melmoth is a living contradiction. He has parted company with the fundamental conditions of life; his bodily organs can no longer sustain his thought. And that is why his laughter freezes and wrings his entrails. It is a laugh which never sleeps, like a malady which continues on its way and completes a destined course. And thus the laughter of Melmoth, which is the highest expression of pride, is forever performing its function as it lacerates and scorches the lips of the laugher for whose sins there can be no remission (*Ess. Rire,* in *C.E.,* 379).

Such is the implacable aspect, the *anti-humanity,*[9] of consciousness in evil. Its constantly accelerated energy seeks an issue outside the limits of man; now it is man, the self-destroyer, who is at once this energy and the limits that he sets for it. The other aspect of consciousness, the *self-purification,*[9] is on the contrary the only possible analogy of salvation at the heart of the ineluctable damnation. "Out of the living spectacle of [his] sad misery," man creates for himself an object of love. Considered as spirit, he recognizes himself to be incorruptible, "immovably centered,"[10] says Baudelaire, citing Emerson. Concerning *L'Héautontimorouménos,* the critical edition of *Les Fleurs du*

Mal refers us to this passage from Byron's *Manfred*: "The immortal soul rewards or punishes itself for its virtuous or guilty thoughts; it is at the same time the origin and the end of the evil which is in it" (*F.M.*, 435).[11] Thus, in his eternity, man without recourse does without God, since he is, potentially, God and Satan all together. He can enjoy simultaneously and all alone, his elevation and his damnation: in Lucifer, Satan becomes a dandy. Let us render this justice to Baudelaire: that he is not a dupe of this closed-circuit game, at least when it concerns the connoisseur of hashish, whose euphoric remorse he analyzes. "We have seen that, counterfeiting in a sacrilegious fashion the sacrament of the penitence, at once penitent and confessor, he had given himself a facile absolution, or still worse, that he had drawn from his condemnation a new nourishment for his pride" (*P.A.*, 59) But this opinion does not mean that Baudelaire challenges the cathartic virtue of the "sombre and limpid tête-à-tête." In the unknown Hermes, the latent Lucifer, he has a foreboding of the enigmatic messenger whose word, rectified, reveals to man his true sense and the only salvation that he can attain. And the interpreter, the rectifier of the double meaning, is it not—"the true representative of irony" but also the reformer of nature—Lucifer in a mirror, the dandy?

Or the poet, this "salamandrine spirit"? Himself enigmatic, "with seriousness masked by frivolity," because he knows better than anyone "that a profound poem, but one complicated, bitter, coldly diabolical (in appearance) is less than any other made for eternal frivolity" (letter to Ancelle, February 18, 1866). When Baudelaire proclaims his own infallibility and the "irrefutable" character of what he writes, it is out of hatred "for these reciters of nothing" incapable "of explaining the meaning of a single word" that they use (*ibid.*). It is easy to understand that the infallibility of the poet is linked to his ambiguity, to the enigmatic nature of his word. This fundamental ambivalence, within which the poet finds his equilibrium infallibly through the exercise of the symbol with the double meaning, constitutes a psychic field so enchanting that a great artist is self-sufficient with the experience of the depths that he renews there constantly. Within these limits—and on the condition of not breaking them; for, outside them, he is damned without recourse—"the artist is responsible only to himself"; he is *his king, his priest and his God.*" How is he related to the dandy? Like him, moreover, is he not his own victim? Priest for himself, Baudelaire consecrated himself early to this role, as is proven by the last stanza of a youthful poem, dedicated to his old classmate Henri Hignard, in which he sings of the soul in its interior enclosure,

> Like a religious monument closed by its priest,
> When night has descended over our somber rooftops,
> When the crowd has departed from the streets,
> Is filled with silence and meditation.

Victim, sacrificer, and sanctuary of oneself—what does the poet lack in order to be unalterably centered in himself? To be his own God. If Baudelaire takes refuge behind Banville in order to go to the full limit of his logic, it is by a humor for which one is grateful to him, but which does not involve his deification: "I am touched by the marvels and the magnificence that the poet decrees in favor of whoever touches the lyre. I am happy to see the absolute divinization of the poet thus posed, without circumlocution, without modesty, without circumspection" (*A.R.,* 356).

Anyway, it is fitting to place the cult of self back in the context of this great destiny. Fallen and a dandy, Baudelaire sets himself up as god in the center of his fall, through a continual vigilance that is also a tireless effort at creation. What he divinizes is this *I,* greater than our I, which constitutes the veritable identity, the excellence of the spirit through the vicissitudes of its never ending transformations. Being conscious, in evil, of the original sublimity of Lucifer, to force oneself "to become what is called a great model of grandeur" (letter to his mother, August 11, 1862) is to remove, as much as possible, the memory of this grandeur from the matter that swallows it up and corrupts it. In truth, in the choice of means, Baudelaire is often trapped in his ambivalence: he would like to be invested, in a sudden flash, with all the energy of Satan to rectify formal creation, to reestablish the true hierarchy of it. Whence his desire, often repeated, for a magic force, that he would use beneficently. "I feel myself to be master of my tool, master of my thought and I have my brain filled with order. If I could on my own have the *Devil in the Flesh* every day, I should be the foremost of men" (to his mother, January 20 25, 1860). To have this on his own, and not with the help of the Devil who is in him. That is clear: instead of giving himself over to this latter by the expedient of the drug, "not only one of the most terrible and the surest means which the Spirit of darkness has at his disposal to enlist and enslave deplorable humanity, but even one of its most perfect incorporations" (*P.A.,* 49), it is a question of subduing the Devil in oneself, of *rehabilitating* him in a way through the creative continuity of an asceticism, diametrically opposed to the discontinuous and destructive processes of magic. The study on *Les Paradis Artificiels* is then based on necessity, and constitutes a decisive debate in Baudelaire's spiritual evolution. It is through the analysis of the progress of the drug and the reverse progress of the drug, that the poet discovers—or formulates clearly—the nature and the means of authentic inner life, the life he intends to lead in poetry. This yields some of the most beautiful pages of his work, such as this testimony that Baudelaire, faced with the magicians of the moment, gives for himself and his kind:

> These wretched souls who have neither fasted nor prayed, and who have refused redemption through work, seek from black

magic the means of suddenly attaining supernatural life. They are deceived by magic and it reveals to them a false happiness and a false light; while we, poets and philosophers, have regenerated our souls through continuous work and contemplation; through assiduous exercise of the will and permanent nobility of intention, we have created for our usage a garden of true beauty. Confident in the word which says that faith moves mountains, we have accomplished the only miracle for which God has granted us license (*P.A.*, 69).

IV. God's Part

1. A Divine Memento: Art or Religion?

Beauty is a miracle then, but *in petto:* God grants to artists the power—more exactly, "the license"—to create for themselves for their own usage "a garden of true beauty," a paradise of replacement, though it be of pure nostalgia. Does this paradise contradict the general law of the fall? No, it is only a human "miracle," which has nothing to do with an act of God carried out through man. Beauty partakes of a natural ambivalence; it is the crowning glory of it, the supreme testimony. It is a travestied religion, and a religious travesty: incessant and desperate reviviscence of an ineffable Memory, *incognito* of a Reality the veritable religious intuition of which attests on the contrary that it is eternally and directly creative among us. Baudelairian art revives sempiternally the fatality of a loss; it maintains the delectation of the irreparable, the distress of the irremissible, while religious hope proclaims man redeemed, original sin atoned. One conceives then that this art is inseparable from a suffering that the artist looks upon as being a contradictory sign of the value of his asceticism and of the unfathomable character of his damnation. Such an art by nature partakes of the eternal, but of an eternal definitively alienated, of which the suffering of the artist is ecstasy. There is something like a negative felicity in suffering.

> For truly, Lord, the clearest proofs
> That we can give of our nobility,
> Are these impassioned sobs that through the ages roll,
> And die away upon the shore of your Eternity.
>
>   (*Les Phares.*)

Where does this inherent limit for art come from, a limitation that Baudelaire perceived with a singular intensity, he who, Fondane saw it clearly, "makes desperate efforts to break the enchanted circle of art"? From the fact that art, for Baudelaire as much and more than for Gautier, is "a *fatum,*" and "its duty an *obsession*" (*A.R.,* 163). The sacrifice that it requires is "involuntary," but conscious; it is, ineluctable and all the more rigorous, a form of consciousness in evil. "On this poor earth where perfection itself is imperfect," the motive, the propulsive force of Beauty is the sentiment dual and one of perfection beyond the attainable and the unbearable imperfection—sentiment in which one recognizes a variant of remorse. "Ah! must we suffer eternally, or flee from beauty eternally? Nature, enchantress without pity, rival always victorious, leave me alone! Cease tempting my desires and my pride! The study of beauty is a duel in which the artist cries out in fright before being conquered" (*Le Confiteor de l'artiste, P.P.P.*). Here Baudelaire means by *nature* the "dictionary" of absolute symbols: immensity, profundity, limpidity, immutability, the thought of which awakens the covetousness of the infinite in the heart of man. Tempting symbols, for they draw toward the gulf. The ambiguity of nature is that it "shivers with a supernatural and galvanic shiver" (*H.E.*) but that this satanic supernatural must be extracted from the very gulf of its seduction by a spirit which, from the fact of remorse, is vanquished in advance.

In *Hymne à la Beauté,* a masterpiece of ambiguous celebration, Beauty is suddenly presented, with an irony which reduces to the absurd the antithesis of the context, like the mediocre reflection of a reflection, an illusion disproportionately enlarged by the miniscule I which gives it to itself in order to enlarge itself:

> The dazzled moth flies toward you, O candle!
> Crepitates, flames and says: "Blessed be this flambeau!"

But even in this case, art is a "purifier like fire" (*Ess. Rire,* in *C.E.,* 404). No matter what the source is from which the light seems to emanate, the approach of this light consumes the one who, in it, thinks he is contemplating infinity. Beauty is then an essence that the artist seeks, with his whole being, to capture in a form, which is never anything except the inadequate symbol of the ardor that he has spent in creating it. This essence consumes the one who becomes enamored of it, more surely destructive than animal concupiscence:

> O Beauty, ruthless scourge of souls, you desire it!
> With the fire of your eyes, brilliant as festivals,
> Burn these tatters which the beasts spared!
> > (*Causerie.*)

Once again the ambiguity appears in the word *fléau,* which can be understood as an ineluctable calamity, or as an instrument to flail grain. This last meaning brings us close to one of the most strangely beautiful images of *Une Charogne,* evoking the cadaver crawling with worms:

> And this world gave forth singular music,
> Like running water or the wind,
> Or the grain that winnowers with a rhythmic motion
> Shake in their winnowing baskets.

To sort the remains is also to sort the seed: yet another image of this haunting sempiternity which makes of the series of existences a succession of only partially materialized forms of the anterior reality, lost forever. Indefinitely, desire for essence drives one to attempt a new shape, to sink even further in formal creation. However, this desire for essence, considered in the absolute, outside the form that it creates, partakes of the sufficient nature of essence itself.

> Poetry, if only one is willing to descend into himself, to interrogate his soul, to recall his memories with enthusiasm, has no other end except itself; it can not have any other, and no poem will be so great, so noble, so truly worthy of the name of poem, as that one which has been written solely for the pleasure of writing a poem (*A.R.*, 157).

The defense by Baudelaire of art considered as its own end, to the exclusion of Truth and Beauty, is too well known and continues to exercise too great an influence for me to insist on it. The distinction of the three orders is not moreover always perfect in it, and appears only when Baudelaire feels himself hindered by the scholasticism of definitions. To differentiate truth from beauty by saying that one analyzes whereas the other seizes the whole, leaves us a little dissatisfied. A more pertinent remark, although it confuses truth and the logical object, can be read in the Preface to the *Nouvelles Histoires extraordinaires:*

> Rhythm is necessary for the development of the idea of beauty, which is the greatest and most noble aim of the poem. Now, the artifices of rhythm are an insurmountable obstacle to this scrupulous development of thoughts and expressions which have truth for their object (*N.H.E.*, 16).

This formal restriction corresponds to the mental cleavage between imagination and understanding, and also between spirit and matter, or even between mercy and justice, a schism with which modern thought is encumbered. Baudelaire, perhaps without suspecting it, drew the hypothesis, however, in an admirable definition of the Imagination, "this queen of faculties," a definition which is found in the *Salon de 1859,* and which is applied point by point to the integral, rational function, to *ardent reason,* to reason psychically founded. It remains that the distinction, impoverishing for one and the other, of the idea of beauty and of that of truth, brings water to the mill of Baudelairian ambiguity, by the cleavage produced thus in the real.

This division all the way into the mind of Baudelaire makes equivocal that which seems the most certain in him, his "mystical" belief in art. We have seen it comprised of antitheses that no integrative faith resolves. Art can be at once objectively deceiving and subjectively authentic: "It is for mortal hearts a divine opium" *(Les Phares),* a sensual pleasure which reminds one of that which Baudelaire, before Legros' *Angélus,*[1] attributes to "the child of the poor," who "tastes, in trembling, the celestial confiture," this spiritual gourmandise analogous to the unrefined extract of hashish. The intoxicating and deceptive substance, although divine, is—no matter what its nature—the outcry of art in the breaking of the ban.

> These curses, these blasphemies, these lamentations,
> These Te Deums, these ecstasies, these cries, these tears,
> Are an echo repeated by a thousand labyrinths—

The echo, the stirring of an absolute loss, reverberated through these personal labyrinths where each one is closed for himself, but where only a few have the awareness of being so: roads-prisons whose exit always disappears, and from which Icarus tried to escape by the well known, fatal means. Now this echo, while enclosing the one that it fills, gives to him the feeling of finiteness where he is broken, and of infiniteness where he is lost. All forms of the revolt and of the imploration are mingled in a crescendo of

blasphemies in the *Te Deum;* outbursts from *Les Phares,* cries
from beings who have gone astray at the frontiers, calls in hate of
limitation, addressed to the limitless, but which, while exalting
those who utter them, do not attain this other sovereign Reality
adorned or hated, the object, conscious or not, of their aim. If
they do not attain it, is it not that a division of principle isolates
them from it and makes of them, not creatures united to God in
prayer, but guilty, rebellious or supplicating, witnesses of *their
dignity* in face of eternity which judges them? How confused is
the ambiguity introduced by these words: "divine opium," recalling this "dose of natural opium" which each one has at his
disposal! One is justified in asking himself if God even, in the
last stanza of *Les Phares,* is not evoked as a pure hallucinatory
expression so that a dignity, without Him relative or absurd, can
be raised in His Face to the absolute.

That Baudelaire makes God play one or several *rôles* in his
ritual theater does not always signify that God is merely a
symbolic projection, but only that Baudelaire's religiosity is of an
order less spiritual than psychic, ill separated, if at all so, from the
conflicts in which he struggles. In a mental world less objectified,
more sensitive than that of his time to the reality of the imaginary, the ambivalence of Baudelairian religious symbolism would
have been less conspicuous, and the poet would have perhaps
been freed from the guilt that it carries. As it is, this ambivalence
is too often radical, and it involves too many consequences so far
as the nature and orientation of art are concerned for it to be
identified and brought out by analysis. But analysis can do it
honestly, *in vivo,* only by submitting as much as possible to the
"queen of faculties," ardent reason, the imagination. For concerning this, with Baudelaire, it is fitting to say: "As it created the
world (one can indeed say so, I believe, even in a religious sense),
it is just that it govern it" (*C.E.,* 274). I emphasize *even in a
religious sense.* Baudelaire feels that God, in his all-creating

freedom, is pure imagination: he maintains also, in spite of the fall, his own imagination to be a living remnant of this primitive freedom. This leads us to the examination, no longer of the illusory nature of art, but of its reality and fundamental veracity, of which it happens that Baudelaire invokes God as a guarantor. A prose poem, *A une heure du matin,* which could have just as well been a part of the *Journaux Intimes,* shows us how Baudelaire's religiosity converges and culminates in the exercise of art:

> Unhappy with all and unhappy with myself, I should really like to redeem myself and be elated a little in the silence and the solitude of night. Souls of those whom I have loved, souls of those whom I have celebrated, make me strong, sustain me, separate me from the deceit and corruptive vapors of the world; and you Lord my God! grant me the grace to produce a few beautiful lines which may prove to me that I am not the lowliest of men, that I am not inferior to those whom I despise.

Certainly, here as always, Baudelaire is haunted by the idea of redeeming himself in his own sight, of proving himself to himself. The dandy reiterates the duty of his status—in a tone of pitiable failure. He cries out his need for recourse to the beloved creatures, and through them, to God himself, in view of accomplishing the law of art. Thus God, sun of the spirits, is confessed as the admirable Principle of which the visible, *on the condition of being seen,* is the lexicon and the image. No matter what his religious fluctuations, Baudelaire founded his aesthetic and his entire work on this conviction of a symbolic reason of things. Sartre is quite free to gloss over in a few words "the rather vague idea of correspondences," and to see in the artist, *unilaterally,* a Narcissus who would be reflected in things, being careful "to show them only through a thickness of human consciousness . . . so that he could easily hold forth on a *Discours sur le peu de réalité* of this exterior world," as if the reality was not indivisibly symbolic, if only from the fact that we are present in it. There exists an art of "vague" things that Sartre does not know about or refuses to consider—one scarcely knows on what grounds—and that is the *intuitive experience,* of which the affective and spiritual criteria are moreover no less rigorous than those of systematic intelligence. That this latter intelligence does not know intelligence of the other sort is a failure, not a superiority. Baudelaire has carefully set the limits of this mysterious knowledge, according to the extent of certain innate qualities: "We know that symbols are obscure only in a relative manner, that is to say according to the purity, the good will or the native clairvoyance of souls" (*A.R.,* 305). These qualities, which are moral in the highest sense of the word, are only the expression of a symbology, itself innate, which institutes them. Thus the order of visible relationships is in a way innervated by that of invisible relations, a conception which can even, in Plotinus, be extended to the three superimposed worlds. For Swedenborg, theoretician of the correspondences, the verbal representation of spiritual things and that of natural things are in the same mystical relation as these things themselves. This mystique of the word leads to a prophetic interpretation, without which man goes his way here below blindly, led astray by representations. Inversely, in *Les Aveugles,* Baudelaire questions himself on the object they seek with their eyes lifted up toward heaven. He confesses, in *La Voix:*

> That very often I take facts for lies
> And that, my eyes raised heavenward, I fall in holes . . .

which seems to imply a separation between the visible and the invisible, a double reading incompatible with unity. Other texts suggest a difference of mental concentration, a faculty for dream unfolding on several levels. Certain chains of impressions or symbolic associations, and the study that the poet makes of the methods producing them, announce Proust and psychoanalysis.

The infallible instrument of such knowledge is the intelligence, "a quasi-divine faculty, which perceives, first of all, outside philosophical methods, the intimate and secret relations of things, the correspondences and the analogies"; a faculty founded on the creative act of God, which Baudelaire seems to conceive as being unique and determinative once and for all. The system of correspondences is then the structure of the world such as God thought it, "things being always expressed by a reciprocal analogy, since the day when God put forth the world like a complex and indivisible totality" (*A.R.,* 206). Universal analogy in its primordial perfection is Paradise: this once lost, correspondences, fragmented but not completely annihilated, are found in the universe of the fall. Art is a means of preserving their memory, without hope of recreating the unity which is broken, but in order to arouse nostalgia for it. Woman—a myth linked by the poet to his conception of the imaginary and art—also plays a contradictory role, as the source and mirage of analogies, as the magician of Remorse and the wetnurse of the nostalgic appetite. But the true place of this nostalgia is nature in its entirety, from top to bottom: "The one who is not capable of depicting everything [. . .] from the visible all the way to the invisible, from Heaven to hell, that one, I say, is not truly a poet in the broad sense of the word and according to the heart of God" (*A.R.,* 308).

According to the heart of God. Must we understand: according to the love that God brings to the world? This notion does not appear in Baudelaire. Rather let us understand: beginning with the center, with the One, and all the way to the extreme of multiplicity in all directions. The immense vastness and the heart are reciprocal: diastole and systole of the Being, in *Eureka* of E. A. Poe. But the center is also the abyss. The mystical euphoria of art, described by the poet in *Élévation* and in certain passages from the study on Wagner, is sometimes the beautiful falsehood of it; in any case it is not its summit. Another thing incomparably more elevated, a knowledge of presentiment can be attained, in the ecstasy of an irremediable misfortune:

> It is this admirable, this immortal instinct of Beauty which makes us consider the earth and its spectacles as a *correspondence* of Heaven. The insatiable thirst for all that lies beyond, and that life reveals, is the most vigorous proof of our immortality. It is both by poetry and through poetry, by and *through* music, that the soul catches a glimpse of the splendors situated beyond the tomb; and when an exquisite poem brings tears to our eyes, these tears are not proof of an excess of joy, they are indeed rather the testimony of provoked melancholy, of a postulation of the nerves, of a nature exiled in imperfection and which would like to secure immediately, on this earth even, a paradise laid bare (*A.R.,* 159).

Baudelaire's God—would he be, as Sartre wishes, only one of the poles of his revery? Concerning this metaphysical and cosmic vision, *supernatural* in the sense in which the poet understands this word, is the image based on nature an equivocal entity, sometimes woman and sometimes Beauty; and is the abode beyond all attainment the *God of correspondences* as Baudelaire thought? Would God be, in short, alternately the interdictor and the forbidden Reality, in an obsessive psychic game, a kind of ineluctable tautology? Did Freud not say, and does Laforgue not apply it to Baudelaire, that "religion is a collective obsession, and obsession an individual religion"? A fine formula, but itself tautological, since it arises from the arbitrary identity of religion and obsession. Even in conceding that obsession has its ritual, the absurdity of this brilliant sentence is that the word *religion* has in it no meaning definable by the author. Religion is the recognition of a principle which transcends our psychic states: it ceases to be if it is confused with revery. But revery can be nourished in it, and religion stretches its roots out into psychism. It may be that the awareness of the fall in Baudelaire and his longing for paradise had been the object of a religious apprehension before he formed a religious idea of God. This God was pleased for a long time to dwell in him in the state of imaginary symbol and idea, incessantly taken back up and questioned in the hope of resolving the enigma of the loss and the fall. But the idea and the symbol were living, and certainly not in Baudelaire alone: in one beyond himself, in a specific, collective existence. "Theocracy and communism. Advice to noncommunists. All is common, even God" (*J.I.*, 88). And if one grant that God does exist, that he is living, which is no more absurd and is infinitely less so than to grant it as specific revery, one must likewise admit that every thought on him is exercised in him—in other words, that no speculation on God is entirely without God. What Baudelaire says of God, he says first to himself and, in a certain manner, to God, revealing thus, under the grill of his particular destiny, the vicissitudes of an indissociable quest and refusal.

We have attempted to decipher this grill, to show how everything in it was arranged with the feeling of a loss, of a fall, both foreshadowed in their spiritual dimensions through an experience which dominates variously a whole life. Baudelaire believes *totally* in what Jouve calls "fundamental death," in original sin: it is even, in the degradation that he experiences, his principle of negative unity. But this symbol corresponds only in part to the Christian notion of the same name; for Baudelaire, the fall does not follow the creation, *it is* the creation. A poem such as *Châtiment de l'Orgueil* presents, it is true, the traditional Christian image of punished pride reiterating the satanic rebellion. The fault of the "most learned doctor," "panic stricken," seized by the call of the great Pan, is to have called himself the progenitor of the man-God and, if he would like, his abortionist. By forcing the divine secret, he claimed to appropriate for himself the principle of all creation—whence the precipitation in him of a chaos which reproduces an image of the world which is common in *Les Fleurs du Mal*.

A crepe of mourning veiled the brilliance of that sun;
Complete chaos rolled in and filled that intellect,
A temple once alive, ordered and opulent,
Within whose walls so much pomp had glittered.
Silence and darkness took possession of it
Like a cellar to which the key is lost.

If this image is a Christian one, it is with elements brought to bear upon it. The sun which veils itself in the first line could be the Swedenborgian *anima,* the inner being communicating to the external intelligence the light of the spiritual sun. The obscured *anima,* cut off from intelligence, becomes precisely this "despised fetus" to which the satanic pride boasted of being able to reduce God. The intelligence, formerly the temple of eternal correspondences, is now the fall itself, in which rolls a world reduced to chaos by the usurpation of the creative Word. As soon as it is broken, the link between human word and the Word of God, the key to universal correspondence, is lost; man falls, enclosed in himself as in his tomb. Thus purely human creation is destruction of the plan of God. What falls into bits is man destined to reunite all the heavens, this *maximus homo* of Swedenborg whose image seduced Baudelaire. For this integral man in whom God would realize his own idea, is substituted fallen man for whom God is incommunicable. God, "the solitary one par excellence," becomes effectively then one of the poles—but the inaccessible pole—of revery. Is it, moreover, less inaccessible than the other pole, matter, represented by woman of whom we know that Baudelaire makes "a creature terrible and incommunicable like God": the one because he is the All beyond all, the other because she is nothing, this nothing being the very mystery of matter?

Completely beyond attainment as these two poles are, man fallen, and thereby full of desire, does not cease reaching out to both, but in opposite fashions, according to whether the physical attraction or the aspiration of the spirit moves him. Matter gives him the illusion of satisfying his appetite for reintegration, since it is plastic to the vain images of unity that he impresses in it. On the contrary, the sovereign beauty of God resides in his pure inaccessibility, beyond all illusion. "To surround oneself exclusively with the seductions of physical art is to create great chances of perdition" (*A.R.*, 294), wrote the poet in *L'Ecole Païenne* (1852), where spiritual passion is added to bitter irony toward the adepts of *art for art's sake*, who prefer to the adoration of "a hanged villain" (*ibid.*, 292) that of Isis and of Osiris. In truth, certain lines could be turned against him, whose art is a mystical fanaticism in which sometimes "the entire man vanishes." But the text as a whole testifies to his fidelity to the values of the "preceding, Christian and philosophical society" (*ibid.*, 294), a definition sufficiently lacking in precision to leave the field free to nostalgia. "May religion and philosophy return one day, as if forced by the cry of one in despair!" (*ibid.*, 295). In writing that, Baudelaire is thinking of Christianity—of a Christianity which would be compatible with his analogical faculty, his imagination. Is he thinking of God and, if so, how?

God transcends religion, but is he necessary for it? Under the influence of Joseph de Maistre, Baudelaire was able to conceive religion as a universal psychic form, venerable in itself. "Even if God did not exist, Religion would still be Holy and *Divine*. God is the only being who, in order to reign, does not even need to exist" (*J.I.*, 7). The idea of God is self-sufficient, even if born of man, and religion is "the greatest *fiction* of the human mind" (*C.E.*, 286). Baudelaire corrects, but significantly: "I speak expressly as an atheistic professor of fine arts would speak, and nothing must be concluded from it against my faith" (*ibidem*). What he venerates in the religious form is both its antiquity and its newness, its eternity. Religion integrates the diversity of the relations that man has always maintained with the invisible part of himself and the universe; it is then for Baudelaire a global, maternal image of the ineffable lost unity. Image greater than the greatest images of art, because it is the fruit not of the genius of a single one but of a long collective sagacity, that of great common-places; and "these wretched ones" do not understand this [. . .], those who believe that a doctrine is made the way a baby is made, on a mattress, *Compère Mathieu*[2] in hand, and that it is no more difficult than that" (*Œ.P.,* I, 243). But whatever may be the antiquity of a doctrine, Baudelaire, following Joseph de Maistre here again, makes it come out of a unique matrix whose ubiquity he describes in this manner:

> Nothing of the eternal and universal needs to be acclimated. This moral analogy of which I spoke is like the divine mark of all un-popular fables. It will be indeed if one wishes, the sign of a unique origin, the proof of an irrefragable kinship, but on the condition that one seek this origin only in the absolute principle and origin of all creatures . . . Myth is a tree which grows every-where, in all climates, under all suns, spontaneously and without having to be propagated by cuttings. The religions and poetries of the four corners of the world furnish us on this subject super-abundant proof. Since sin is everywhere, redemption is every-where, myth is everywhere. Nothing more cosmopolitian than the Eternal (*A.R.,* 229-230).

What is this "common origin," absolute principle of all crea-tures? One is obviously tempted to reply: God. But if, in Baude-laire's mind, the fall is identical to creation, the principle of every being is the fall itself. The common origin would be then rather in this memory eternally present of which the invisible obverse side of the coin is the lost Eden; and sin, the visible reverse side of it, the alchemy of thought consisting in evoking the former by the latter. "What is the universal religion? (Chateaubriand, De Maistre, the Alexandrians, Capé). There is a universal religion, made for the Alchemists of Thought, a religion which frees itself from man, considered as a divine memento" (*J.I.*, 86).

Thus, to understand Baudelaire well, it is important to distinguish his *God* from his *religion*. His work, for whoever delves deeply into it, can be read like a masked dialogue with the Inaccessible. As a child, he conversed with the personal God of the catechism and of his mother, pious as he was still at twenty on one side of his nature, the other showing faintly the traits of Cramer. But if the awakening of his poetic faculty does not efface his religiosity, it metamorphoses it and integrates it into art like one of its contradictory elements. God becomes a poetic object, hidden moreover, removed. Between the twentieth and the thirtieth year of the poet, while his great themes are taking shape, God appears there, generally just beneath the surface of a visionary philosophy having an obvious psychic content. For a long time identical to the Platonistic One, this God will take a providential form when the poet feels the need; we shall see this in the last years. As to Baudelaire's religion, it is a kind of fundamental mythology, the irreducible canvas of the great enigmas of the spirit and of the spirit as enigma which envelops them: a mythology which *frees itself from man,* for whom it is like the ancestral Dream, and the Memorial of his origin. About this religion we could say, by modifying Freud's word, that it is a specific obsession. For Baudelaire, who concedes along with de Maistre that "entire man is only a malady," this absolute malady is *ipso facto* of a religious nature. To say that the *entire* man is only *a* malady, is to assume evil to be in the very essence of the *human being:* religion, the obsession of essential evil, is also, reciprocally, the obsession to purify essence. "As sin is everywhere, redemption is everywhere, *myth is everywhere."* Myth: imaginary operation completely immanent, of which the "moral dynamics" activate, simultaneously, "sin" and "redemption," postulations which are self-sufficient. "Religion" such as Baudelaire understands it, is the exhaustive, "absolute" experience, extreme psychic states corresponding to these two postulations—experience in which man himself saves himself, without ceasing all the same to fall.

2. *A Highly Suspect Catholic*

We are here far from the Mystery of the Redemption such as Christianity reveals it. *Châtiment de l'Orgueil* and *Le Reniement de Saint Pierre* aside, Baudelaire, in all his work, makes only some twenty allusions to Jesus and not one directly to his role of redeemer. Twice, it is true, the Resurrection is evoked. "It is there (said the poet about Jerusalem) that Death was trampled under foot, it is also there that it opened up its most sinister crater" (*P.A.,* 169). Rembrandt-like image: a focal symbol is discerned, shining and dark. What is its role in real belief? All his life and with more insistence at the end, Baudelaire ridiculed those who make a mythological figure out of Jesus, and also those who see in him only *a great man,* the *"lawgiver of Christians"* (*Œ.P.,* I, 222). He himself, in *Examen de Minuit,* after having confessed in a first version:

> We have blasphemed Jesus,
> The most lovable of all the Gods!

replaced the second line with this one, having an affirmative irony: "The most undeniable of all the Gods." Christ, in his eyes, is "the eternal crucified one above the crowd" (*Œ.P.,* III, 193), the Word of whom, remembering Joseph de Maistre, he declares in *De l'Essence du Rire:* "The sage par excellence, the Word incarnate, never laughed" (*C.E.,* 372). Is this incarnate Word which, however, "has known anger, [. . .] has even known tears" (*ibid.*), a living, concrete being, the Christ of the Gospels? Is it not rather, transposed by Baudelaire's imagination, a symbol opposed to the one of Melmoth: in all his perfection, the Resemblance in which all men are brothers, man considered as *divine memento?*

> In the terrestrial paradise (whether one supposes it passed or to come, memory or prophesy, as theologians or socialists), in the terrestrial paradise, that is to say in the milieu in which it seemed to man that all things created were good, joy was not in laughter (*C.E.,* 373).

A witness of the lost Paradise, Christ such as he appears in *Révolte* comes to teach men to reconquer through the beatitudes this spiritual Eden. If he succumbs to the universal mockery that is Evil unchained absolutely by his immaculate being, it is as a fatal victim, an involuntary one: vain victim, since this non-addressed sacrifice is scoffed at by divine arbitrariness. "The one who in his heaven laughed at the sound of the nails" is himself a fallen God, since he laughs. No more than man, God is not without loss: in the cosmic drama, Jesus alone is innocent, and thereby, precisely, absurd; he can save neither man, nor God. Like Melmoth, but in a different order, he is *a living contradiction,* which reunites a divinity precipitated into the abyss and a Humanity elevated to Heaven—an idea far removed from the Christian Man-God, and from the redemptive operation. "Docile Martyr, condemned innocent one"; just as, in *Le Léthé,* the lover of the woman-matter, the Jesus of *Révolte,* reminds us of Melmoth's Immalee. He remains the poetic figure par excellence, the highest of these creatures of light whom "the blind Angel of expiation seized."

That, doubtlessly, is the image of Jesus which emerges from *Le Reniement de Saint Pierre,* for one who takes this poem at face value. But the ignorance, little compatible with his formation, that the poet displays in it concerning doctrines and the sacrifice of the Cross, arouses the idea of a complex dialectic. Is the poem what it appears to be? Does it wish not to give rise to scandal but to give the image of a scandal? Literally it is a fine piece of rhetoric on a well known Romantic theme. The divinity—written with a small letter—is reduced in it to an attribute of "immense Humanity"—with a capital letter. According to human logic (that of the poem under its literal light), Jesus betrayed his Humanity by not appropriating for himself his strength from God to carry out the work of Man in *a world where action would be the sister of dream*. On the one hand the admirable evocation of the punishment reveals abundant compassion for eternal Man ("the eternal crucified one") in a Jesus dissociated from the work of the Father and having only the name of Son: on the other, this compassion takes on resentment with respect to this same Jesus who, having come "to carry out the eternal promise," is only a supreme hobgoblin set up by paternal jealousy. If there is promise of reintegration, of *recapitulation,* it cannot come from the anthropophagic God such as the poem depicts him. *Révolte* lets us have a presentiment that Satan made this promise of accomplishment for himself, and that it is enclosed in the state of "grievous secret" in our incurable nostalgia. *All happens as if* Baudelaire were reproaching Jesus for not being Satan: to have expiated for man, or for God himself, instead of making God expiate.

Thus the greatest poet of suffering symbolizes its contradictory aspects. This expiation, which man blesses as long as he considers its rectification as a grace, he regards as a jealous vengeance when he sets himself up against an unacceptable divine anger. In this last case, suffering appears at the same time like the stigmata of divine arbitrariness and the goad of demonic ambition. The one who refuses in us is Satan, the fallen man who makes for himself an absolute of his fall, and who takes his suffering, knowingly exacerbated, as the excuse for an endless revolt. But to refuse can be first of all to feel oneself rejected, expelled. Such a revolt sets man up at once against a divine Will identified with Evil and against the interest of man himself who rejects this identification.

To the contrary of a Hugo who "believes that man is born good, and yet, even faced with his permanent disasters, [. . .] does not profess the ferocity and malice of God" (*A.R.,* 391), rebellious man believes Evil to be consubstantial with God as with man. To revolt is to snatch suffering from the hands of God, to appropriate it definitively for one's own usage, to take upon oneself, absolutely, boundless suffering for the condition and the inherent Evil in Life. To supplant God, man will break at the price of this infinite suffering all the terrors and limitations of suffering. Toward the top as toward the bottom, this world must be totally without love, which implies an indefatigable effort of suffering to destroy love as divine form. Psychic projection or very real enemy, God becomes the inverse image of the horror that man lives and transcends: satanic derision, blasphemy, jealousy, remorse, terror. "A mocking God," intoxicated with our "flood of anathema," a "God jealous" of the "clear eye" of Satan, a God with the "terrible claw," sometimes, however, "touched with remorse." It is, personalized, objectified, the destructive principle lodged in man. Essentially a castigator, this God that must be vanquished is the *Father,* the *bad double* of Satan the liberator celebrated in *Les Litanies:*

> Adopted father of those whom in black rage
> God the Father drove from the earthly paradise.

In this same poem, the myth of man self-creator is constantly read just beneath the surface, to reveal his sacrilegious resolution in the final lines of *Abel et Caïn:*

> Race of Cain, ascend to heaven,
> And cast God down upon the earth!

To culminate the work of revolt, "the eternal promise" is projected, in the *Prière* of *Les Litanies de Satan* in the vision of a magically restored paradise, a Temple of correspondences erected again, which would be nothing more than the sanctuary of Satan, the Tree of Knowledge. Thus the *maximus homo* would be Man Satan, and the entire story of the fall would be reversed.

> Grant that my soul may someday repose near to you
> Under the Tree of Knowledge, when, over your brow,
> Its branches will spread like a new Temple!

Such is, at a certain depth, the dialectical movement of Baudelaire between God and Satan. In more obscure depths, removed from the influence of contemporary themes, this movement perhaps has its contrary, linked to it in inverse reciprocity. Pierre Jean Jouve, the admirable analyst of Baudelaire, sees in *Les Litanies de Satan* "the absolute reversal of a religious attitude." Must we accept the intuition of the same writer, "that Satan is God having found it necessary to undergo a disguise"? On this point, the alibi of the "travestied religion" (letter to Ancelle, February 18, 1866) is rich in ambiguities, the first of which: is it an alibi or not? The letter to Ancelle is only a great cry from the poet incarcerated in a misunderstanding of which he does not know if he is author or victim: nothing isolates poets more than this language by preterition which comes from their intuitive nature. Speaking no doubt about *Les Fleurs du Mal,* Baudelaire wrote thus, enigmatically: "God is a scandal—a scandal which produces" (*J.I.,* 26). The poet of *Les Fleurs du Mal,* as we know, expected from this book a *yield*—financial *yield,* it is understood, but which would have been only the sign of another. He was counting on "universal intelligence" to stumble on the horror of the evil through its sacriligeous seductions, and draw a salutary effect from their frightful beauty. That is at least what he writes in many places, whether this is for his defense or not: we have no reason not to believe him, but, if I dare say so, within the system of his ambiguity. He could not, moreover, be unaware of these passages from the Scripture in which the Messiah appears like a "sign of contradiction" (Luke 2:3),[3] "sanctuary and stumbling-block, trap, snare" (Isaiah 8:14). If one remembers the words of Christ to his disciples, on his way toward the Mount of Olives: "All ye shall be offended because of me this night. (Matt. 26:31), he will read *Le Reniement de Saint Pierre* like the illustration of the eternal offense of Jesus. Beside this thematic justification of the scandal, can one advance a more intimate reason, dependent on the secret of the spirit? By associating God and evil in the offense, does the poet, wittingly or not, resort to the dialectic of blasphemy in order to oust from this latter the true God? *A God whose visible relation with man is through evil: is that not an absolute offense, an indecipherable and yet spiritually vital enigma?* Does this offense not concern man in his secret for the same reason that it concerns God? Is there not, at the heart of the offense, a measure, a proportion of another order, that the offense alone can represent here below? Baudelaire's work is an apparent soliloquy in which he suffocates while struggling against himself and against God, at the very depths of this offense which is its sole object. *L'Irrémédiable* and *Révolte* co-respond to each other: these are the extremes of a vocation. If Baudelaire has not escaped the offense by inventing just any sort of freedom, it is because he was *dedicated to the offense* and, according to all human appearance, was an *accursed being*. And if he personified himself like that for twenty years, it is to answer a requirement that his person aided him in maintaining.

Concerning *Les Fleurs du Mal,* Barbey d'Aurevilly wrote that the poems "are God's justice." They are so in the first place for their poet, *to whom they render justice* by charging him personally with the suffering and the repulsion of the scandal, by making him the *scapegoat.* Baudelaire expresses this vocation thus: "When I have inspired universal disgust and horror, I shall have conquered solitude" (*J.I.*, 26). Conquest in several phases, of which the first is the exterior scandal pure and simple. In making a pariah of Baudelaire, consciousness in evil sets him up against the idea of God who offends him. He is the emissary of this two-sided scandal that the mass of men, and the poet included, see in a God that they make in their image only to be offended or terrified by him. Baudelaire's attitude is not only (although it is that too) a magical provocation, an inverted religious practice. He gives himself the task of exaggerating the offense to the point of making it intolerable for Christians and atheists alike: for Christians, who do not want to see that their moral God is a blasphemy: for atheists, who refuse to see the depth of sin in man, and that it is the abyss of the silence of God. Baudelaire is then alone against all and, first of all, against himself. Then the second phase of the conquest intervenes: the accent of the offense changes from God to man, for whom the word of the enigma is *expiation*.

We have seen many times the bitter and subtle game of reciprocal metamorphoses between "religion" and "counter-religion." The frequence of this game leads one to think that the Christian intuitions of Baudelaire are linked to an unconscious process. Their role is to translate states; even sacrilege becomes a figure. Blasphemous, the metamorphosis does not spare the image of Christ. The second movement of the offense begins by an identification with the Crucified one. The folly of the Cross possesses the poet. Disguised in a hundred different ways, one finds it in the great texts, almost on each page of *Les Fleurs du Mal*, in most of the *Poèmes en prose*, in *De l'Essence du Rire*, in *Les Paradis Artificiels*, in the studies on E. A. Poe. One measures there the impact in his mind of the central words of the Christian life, this for example: "For the Jews require a sign, and the Greeks seek after wisdom: But we preach Christ crucified, unto the Jews a stumblingblock, and unto the Greeks foolishness"

(I Corinthians 1:22–23). Only, if Baudelaire burdens himself with the cross, it is in order to hang himself there in place of Christ; and his cross is his very sin that he commits in order to be crucified. To take upon himself the double crime of God against man and of man against God, is his way of *accepting being a creature*. Thus the two postulations make only one offensively: the two poles of the uncommunicable, God and matter, become objects of a unique movement. An impressive manipulation of the symbol of the Cross appears in *Un Voyage à Cythère*. J. D. Hubert, in a remarkable work, has justly noted that the "gallows with three arms" on which the allegorical image of the poet hangs, is identical to the Cross. We must go further. Christ made himself *sin* for us, says Saint Paul: now the "Cytherean" who hangs on the gallows is sin itself. The punishment of this "poor devil" (note the reference, probably intentional, to Satan) is in every way like that of Christ in *Le Reniement de Saint Pierre*. To the cry of Pascal: "Jesus will be in agony to the end of the world," responds, in Baudelaire, this vision of another "eternal crucified one" and of another eternity of suffering:

> Cytherean, child of a sky so beautiful,
> You endured those insults in silence
> To expiate your infamous adorations
> And the sins which denied to you a grave.

Is the true Baudelairian "Christ" this living corruption, the scapegoat devoted to sempiternal execration and expiation, hanged on the "symbolic gallows" of redemption by the Cross? Is the "image" of the poet, who hangs on this gallows, Satan, sacrificer and victim of his indefatigable black mass, which is celebrated in a rich, full voice on an appreciable number of the most beautiful pages of the work, from *Les Fleurs du Mal* to *Tannhaüser?* The order of the fall would then be without remedy, the expiation offensive and necessary, without redemption or true salvation. It would be nothing more than the fact of assuming silently his destiny in evil. The final cry of the poem is only the more troubling, a turning to God in order to ask him not for a salvation that he cannot or does not wish to grant, but for lucidity in the expiation, hence in evil, unique purification of which the fallen spirit is capable:

—O! Lord! give me the strength and the courage
To contemplate my body and soul without loathing!

As far as the work itself is concerned (with the exception of the intimate notes) this cry is the summit of the vocation in Baudelaire: the poet, *as poet,* has not gone further. He has no less accomplished his task: to symbolize, through the effort of a creative intuition applied to the great images of the fall, this fall and this aspiration that he lived jointly in spirit, alone and yet in the universal singular. The third movement of this conquest of solitude which, in the work, stops at the constat of the irremediable contradiction, would have been the passing beyond the offense, that is to say, in the *nonadulterated* Christian perspective, to the recognition of the mediation of Christ and, in it, of the reinstated human freedom. The benefit of such a great creative effort could have been the definitive autonomy of the spirit, cleansed finally of the antinomies in which God and Satan are reversed, and capable of thrusting aside all arbitrary representation in order to open itself up to its own freedom at the same time as to unfathomable mercy. It does not seem that the poet, *as poet,* ever earned—or received—this supreme freedom, through which God expresses himself in us. It is perhaps that he wished, precisely, to remain a poet, *qua* poet. He did not divine the key of his own enigma: God's *incognito* in him. God is "absent" from the interior soliloquy: even invoked nominally, he is kept beyond reach. Always, in Baudelaire, he remains silent and distant. Neither *Bénédiction* nor *L'Imprévu* invalidates the poems of *Révolte*. The Christian perspective warped by the imagination, but in which Baudelaire the poet entered only by this latter, has not been rectified in his word. To read it, one gets the feeling that rebellion and submission are the alternated moments of a fiction of the solitary conscience, crushed by the weight of Evil and of the Law, and which experiences likewise its dignity either in rising up against God, or in giving to oneself for a righter of wrongs this very God, without finding the escape from the offense in which it is locked.

Such then is the imaginary structure of the debate that the mind carries on with itself through Baudelaire's work. This debate is in a way a "battle of angels," which, certainly, is waged in the soul of the poet, but is carried on in its universal part, indeed its abstract part. It rarely corresponds, in its vicissitudes, to the concrete existence of man: this superconsciousness that spiritual experience is can envelop the ordinary consciousness without ever penetrating it. Without being insincere to any degree, a man can remain quite inferior to his vision—or live it at depths that he is unaware of. The problem which arises for us then could be formulated in this manner: Baudelaire's poetry develops a fundamental symbology of the fall, a symbology implicating man and God, but which seems to exclude all relations with love, all relations except submission or revolt, punishment or damnation. These themes as such are treated by the poet with an unequalled skill. These are the archetypes of the spirit: God himself is one of them, dominating all the others. But let us descend to the plane of daily existence. Is God present there or not? Did Baudelaire intimately feel the presence or absence of a personal God, corresponding or not to his poetic speculation?

This God sometimes comes between the poet and his mother, in the letters addressed to her. Baudelaire treats him most often as an hypothesis, either to dismiss, not without aggressiveness against his mother: *"Then God and heaven with which I have nothing to do"* (letter of December 26, 1853), or to hope that it may be true: "And God! you will say. I desire with all my heart (with what sincerity, no one can know except me!) to believe that an exterior and invisible being is interested in my destiny; but what can I do to believe it?" (letter of May 6, 1861). Let us see the following: "The idea of God makes me think of that cursed priest [the one in Honfleur, his "bête noire"!]. In the sorrowful feelings that my letter is going to cause, I do not want you to go to him. This priest is my enemy, through sheer stupidity perhaps." The interference of this detestable priest—symbol of institutionalized religion, no doubt also of maternal conformity—does not tarnish, however, the religious aspiration. It is true that this aspiration translates an egocentric need for security: Can God be efficacious? When Baudelaire speaks ironically about his mother's prayers: "Your idea of praying to God about my theater affairs is very comical: but everything that comes from you is always good" (letter of October 10, 1859), the irony is not aimed at intercession, but at the content of it, little worthy of an eventual Providence. Baudelaire excludes so little the virtues of intercession, which implies a providential idea, that he cries out thus the need for one: "I am horribly unhappy, and if you believe that a prayer can be efficacious (I speak without jest) pray for me and do so vigorously" (letter to his mother, October 8, 1860). This conception, still hypothetical and utilitarian, of a sustaining Wisdom, antithesis of the "diabolical Providence who prepares misfortune right from the cradle" (*H.E.,* vii), will become stronger through the trials of the last years, and with it, although timidly, the hope of a personal separation will dawn. Belated hope, not founded in grace, simple echo of a desperate urgency, but *hope* of a redemption that Baudelaire *would owe only to himself.* "I have my mind full of funereal ideas. How difficult it is to do one's duty *every day,* without any interruption! [. . .] How many times has God given me credit of a few days! [. . .] Will I have the time (supposing I have the courage) to make amends for all that I have to?" (to his mother, January 1, 1865).

In four years, God then became for Baudelaire *an exterior and invisible being interested in his destiny*—years after the break with Jeanne, years of anguish and illness. The erotic religion is shaken, the rival Idol crumbles. The Mother remains, an intermediary, accepted rather than solicited. That the condition of the poet reduced him to bare distress must not invalidate the value of his belief. The time of the only ontological proof, such as his *Calcul en faveur de Dieu* (*J.I.,* 54) formulated it, has passed. A new experience is given to him, a proof which can be a spiritual threshold. His conception of the mystery—the wretchedness of man, his very own—calls henceforth for a recourse. No matter what one thinks of *Pauvre Belgique!,* written three years before his death, one cannot help being struck by the relentlessness with which the poet vituperates the universal atheism that he attributes to the Belgians. This virile atheism makes him stumble upon the pretentious baseness of man, offense opposed to that of God. Baseness of man who gets along naturally without God; of man who believes himself *naturally* good, born for unlimited progress as announced by industrial inventions. Baudelaire is not far from considering this category of minds as subhuman. But he has a presentiment of it victorious: it has for itself the strength of its limits, and the weight of number to impose them. "It is impossible for a Belgian to believe that a man believes what he himself does not believe" (*Pauvre Belgique!,* in *Œ.P.,* III, 71). The horror that Baudelaire experiences is from a superior mind who sees the mystery jeered at by a foolish "plain common sense." When one thinks of the materialistic virulence of the epoch in which he had "the tiresome good fortune to live" (*Œ.P.,* I, 222), one understands that the disgust of the poet was for him a permanent physical malaise against a background of atrocious spiritual anguish. Doubtlessly he sees then in atheism the worst sign of divine anger, the *unconscious* doing of evil. "The philosophy of these sectarians is now known to us; it can be outlined in this frightful formula: *'The peace of the soul is exhausted in negation of God'* " (*Œ.P.*, III, 113). Now what Baudelaire wishes to express in his bitter book on Belgium "is the raillery of all that is called *progress,* but what I call *the paganism of imbeciles,* and the demonstration of the government of God" (letter to Ancelle, February 18, 1866). But of what government? Is it in the abandonment to his fall that Providence punishes man? A less concise idea of Providence, which corresponds to the evolution of the last years toward belief—if not faith—in a personal God, is sketched out here, unexpected, compressed between two parentheses: "The Christian idea (the God invisible, creator, omniscient, conscious, omni-provident) cannot enter into a Belgian brain" (*Pauvre Belgique!, Œ.P.*, III, 127).

The sentence dates from a time when the apparent concern of the writer is to accumulate notes in order to say the worst things possible about the Belgians. But the choice of these notes is significant: an intense religious reflection orients him, under a camouflage of newspaper clippings. Even confining oneself to *Pauvre Belgique!,* one could analyze the final attitude of Baudelaire in matters of religion. The return to Christianity appears definitive in it; the need for a Providence is equally for a framework. It is then not without interest to look back, toward the years when for the poet religion was dependent on aesthetics more than on definite belief. Fragments of letters, *Fusées,*[4] remarks, often in passing, which are scattered through the critical work, or, more poignant, confidences in *Mon coeur mis à nu,* cause to scintillate with an uneven brilliance the facets of a "catholicism" that one could call "reference catholicism," to which the poet makes an appeal for all purposes, most often as to a passing catalyst, sensorial and even erotic, sometimes as though to a true spiritual place. What was this "catholicism"? What did Baudelaire know about his religion? I would willingly believe that his knowledge of it was variable according to the seasons of his soul and the ambiguities of his spirit. The dialectics of creation could arouse a religious attention of a certain order, *impersonal*, in a closed circuit. Thus, in the poems of *Révolte*, ignorance disguises perhaps, and reveals to the second degree, a formidable intuitive knowledge. I detect in *De l'Essence du Rire* an intuition which, precisely, can be compared to this knowledge. Baudelaire saw there that with Christianity a new threshold is attained with universal consciousness: the intelligence of good and evil is affirmed, the blade of laughter given a sharp edge. "That is why I do not find it astonishing that we, children of a law better than the ancient religious laws, we, favored disciples of Jesus, we possess more comic elements than pagan antiquity. That even is a condition of our general intellectual strength" (*Ess. Rire, C.E.,* 381).

Anyway, this palingenetic consideration hardly informs us about the abundance of the poet's Christian ideas. A note in *Mon coeur mis à nu* says more about it: "Fine conspiracy to organize for the extermination of the Jewish people. The Jews, *Librarians* and witnesses of the *Redemption*" (*J.I.,* 101). Taken as an anti-Semitic outburst, it is in fact, even in its atrocious humor, the ellipsis of the traditional vision of the Mystery of Israel in the economy of the salvation. It could be read just as well coming from the pen of a Léon Bloy, for whom the history of the Jews, this long expectation of a Coming, was a dam obstructing all human history, raising it up thus to make of it the threshold of a Messiah. For those who understand the Baudelairian antiphrasis, the *impossible* and always possible extermination of the Jews, the pouring out "of general animality," could be conceived as a satanic conspiracy in view of hastening an absolute event, of an ambivalent nature, in which some would see the end of Christianity and the triumph of man without God, others the end of time and the last Judgment of history. Readable in both senses, the double sentence of Baudelaire seems to permit only the Christian interpretation: its strength does not fail to astonish us from an author whose theological learning is, apparently, nonexistent or aberrant. The second part could be a reader's note: how, in this case, would the so profound intuition of the debate have been derived from it? Or are the two images, of the permanent testimony of Israel and of the permanent conspiracy against it, born together, in their complex relationship, out of the cruel divination of the genius?

In the poet, divination is inseparable from aesthetic vision: profundity, even religious, has first of all the appearance of a fine effect. Each can lead to the other; the intuition of the profundity can be accepted only in view of the effect, the beauty of which, reciprocally, can incite to profound adhesion. Baudelaire is very conscious of this: "Art is the only spiritual domain where man can say: 'I shall believe if I wish, and, if I do not want to, I shall not believe!'" (*Salon de 1859, C.E.,* 286). To believe, for an artist of his persuasion, is to adhere closely to an image, to inhabit it in spirit. An edifying example of this way of "believing" is found in the remarks of the poet on Delacroix's *Mise au Tombeau:*

> It is impossible for an amateur who is anything of a poet not to feel his imagination struck, not by an historical impression, but by an impression of poetry, religion and universality, as he gazes at that little group of men who are tenderly carrying the body of their God into the depths of a crypt, into that sepulchre which the world will adore, 'the only sepulchre,' as René superbly said, 'which will have nothing to give up at the end of time' (*C.E.,* 294–95).

The preceding is a text in which one seizes the symbolic nature, by the purely imaginary mechanism, of the concept that

Baudelaire works out for himself of one of the great Christian mysteries. An immense religious reality is strongly perceived here, but the spiritual emotion of it is indiscernible from aesthetic pleasure. That is only natural for Baudelaire, who, challenging the theory which considers faith as the unique source of spiritual inspiration, would willingly make the sensibility peculiar to art analogous to religious sentiment: how would he better have illustrated his thought than in citing, apropos of Delacroix, the author of the *Génie du Christianisme?*

Did Baudelaire the poet ever put aside his ambiguity, were it only for a single positive religious affirmation? Apparently not: the psychic submerged all from the very beginning, the aesthetic muddled all. Let one judge it by this other opinion on Delacroix, dating from the youthful years of the poet:

> The grave sadness of his talent is perfectly suited to our religion which is itself profoundly sad—a religion of universal anguish, and one which, because of its very catholicity, grants full liberty to the individual and asks no better than to be celebrated in each man's own language—so long as he knows anguish and is a painter (*Salon de 1846, C.E.,* 113).

Is this algolagnia then in the spirit of religion? Without a doubt, but Baudelaire quite readily declares his own tendency toward melancholy to be a Catholic one. Did he not, in the same manner, play with erotic ambiguity? "This ardent and delicate mysticity which generally blossoms only in the garden of the Roman Church" (*P.A.,* 173), one imagines what its atmosphere is for him to think inhaling it: "Protestant countries lack two elements indispensable for the happiness of a well-brought-up man, gallantry and devotion" (*J.I.,* 27). One can see how, corrupted, the exquisiteness of Marian loves delight the sensual and frustrated child whose appetites extend into manhood. Baudelaire, however, took seriously his aesthetico-sensual "catholicism," consubstantial to his very imagination, differently from his electoral "Catholicism" as a candidate for the Academy. Confessing this academic Catholicism, the poet wrote to Sainte-Beuve that, if he feels himself to be a better "papist" than Villemain, he is nevertheless "a very suspect Catholic." A month earlier, in a letter of solicitation to Laprade, he took pleasure in refining parodoxically the idea of the Catholicism in *Les Fleurs du Mal.* "In supposing that the work is diabolical, does there exist, one could say, anyone more Catholic than the devil?" He was no less convinced that "this book originated from a Catholic idea" (to his mother, April 1, 1861). If Chenavard, the spiritualist painter, "philosopher and subtle reasoner," had laughed at this idea, "never having sensed the Catholicism beneath *Les Fleurs du Mal"* (to V. de Laprade, December 23, 1861), others, beginning with Barbey d'Aurevilly, had detected it or were going to recognize it for the same simple and ambiguous reasons that Baudelaire gave to himself: the sense of sin, that of suffering, the longing for redemption. Perhaps they would agree likewise with his definition of "a being truly *catholic,* in equal communication and relation with all that is above and all that is below, with learned people and noneducated people, with the guilty as with the innocent" (*P.A.,* 95).

The preceding is thus a unified vision of a communion, but a definition without precise substance, as is, in short, *all* of Baudelaire's religion. Take away from it the poet's obsessions, psychic guilt on the one hand, aesthetic revery on the other, there remains the misunderstood vestiges of a forgotten childhood religion. The idea of faith that Baudelaire formulates has no meaning: "Supremacy of the pure idea, with Christians as with the communistic babouvist.[5] Fanaticism of humility. Not even to aspire to understand religion" (*J.I.,* 84). His conception of the three orders of the social hierarchy comes from Maistre, from Platonism, from Tradition, from everything, except Christianity: "Among men only the poet, the priest and the soldier are great. The man who sings, the man who blesses, the man who sacrifices others and himself. The others are made for the whip" (*J.I.*, 81). Baudelaire is suspicious of the priest and the soldier because of his poet's nature, feminine, of an androgynous turn of mind. The Church represents for him, symbolically, the ubiquity of the Feminine Principle: "That the Church wants to do everything and to be everything, is a law of the human spirit" (*J.I.*, 9). "Femininity" in which the priest shares and which he fecundates: "The priest is immense because he makes people believe in a multitude of astonishing things" (*J.I.*, 9). As for the soldier, complement of the priest, he is the paternal image, the Angel of the vengeful God, the witness and guarantee of the ubiquity of war, it too a law of the world. "The true saint is the one who whips and who kills people for the good of the people" (*J.I.*, 18). Priest and soldier, this cosmic couple reiterates the symbolism of childhood. Minister of universal analogy, the priest attests to the eternal return to the womb; instrument of numinous anger, the soldier attests to universal expiation. And the poet, what place does he have between them? The same place as Baudelaire in his childhood, between memory and the forbidden: the passive link and the resonator of their contradictory unity.

Did the amalgam of the psychic and the religious give way, in the last years, to a more coherent religion? What is certain is that the poet declared in Belgium: "I am Catholic and Roman, and I have reflected a great deal on that." His notes prove quite clearly that he did ponder the scandal of atheism. But concerning his religion as an ensemble of symbols and concepts, one remains justified in thinking that it forms a very impure, indeed undefinable, blend. Is the same true concerning his religiosity? Jules Vallès was not mistaken when he wrote, in his violent indictment, before the still warm body: "This braggart of immorality was fundamentally a religious hypocrite." It is that the tone of the work is that of an absolute conviction; it vibrates with a constant spiritual tension. Permeated with the feeling of the irremediable, Baudelaire is no less so with respect to the grandeur of the expiation—ideas designed to displease the "mocking and distrustful epoch" to which Vallès belonged. Consciousness in the evil act constitutes the daily asceticism of the poet: he maintains in it, pure from the corruption of the fall, the dignity of the interior man. Such is, for almost all his life, the essential element of Baudelaire's *piety:* the maceration of an absolute spirit precipitated into an irremissible evil. That the author of the fall be man or God changes nothing with regard to its fatality, and purification through suffering is in view of no transcendent reconciliation or any communion of saints. This travail of the soul through suffering is a completely individual operation, voluntary or not, but quite a lucid one, which, without liberating in any way from the fall, restores the shadow of their innate nobility to the only spirits that make themselves conscious: *self-purification and antihumanity*[6] *(J.I.,* 24). Such a piety would be stoic, if it were more than a passive lucidity, paralyzed by the consciousness of its procrastination; as if the effort of consciousness cancerized moral faith itself, atrophied in addition by the idea of a fall without reprieve. The piety of the dandy in the mirror is summed up in his dress, that of the singularly essential, a constantly exacting and visible recall of an unsatiable identity, which is only the abyss of a nostalgia.

This nostalgia colors all Baudelaire's religiosity: it furnishes him the mystical distance necessary for his imagination in order to rise up and fall. Without any risk, Sartre would say, since the evil is incurable and Eden lost forever. We would be tempted to say it too, were it not for the accent of this nostalgia, by which its very object is communicated. Nostalgia is the reverse side of a spiritual aspiration, why not the negative of a mysterious labor? The irreparable, the uncommunicable, is in a way, the broken absolute. Almost all the themes of the *Petits Poèmes en Prose* could be reduced to this ambiguous constant and to the pleasure of sadness that it procures—complicity of intoxication and despair, that no direct invocation to God breaks. Outside such an invocation, which, in the space of an instant, implicates—there, even where it would best be applied, the whole Baudelairian scheme of alienation and fall—and reintroduces *even into self-creation,* through the bias of an impassioned question, the personal relation to the God who saves:

> Life teems with innocent monsters. Lord, my God! you the Creator, you the Master; you who have made Law and Liberty; you, the sovereign who allows to act, you the judge who pardons; you who are full of reasons and causes, and who have perhaps placed within my mind the taste for horror in order to change my heart, like the cure at the tip of a blade: Lord, have pity on the insane of both sexes! O Creator, can there exist monsters in the eyes of That One alone who knows why they exist, how they *are made* and how they might *not have been made?* (*Mademoiselle Bistouri, P.P.P.*).

Baudelaire's work includes few similar cries. In *Les Fleurs du Mal,* out of four direct addresses to God, there are only two prayers of adoration (in *Bénédiction* and in *L'Imprévu*) giving thanks to him for the gift of suffering. These two texts are likewise the only ones which suggest not only the restoration of original integrity, but (in *L'Imprévu* at least) a new paradisiacal hierarchy based on merits acquired in suffering. Here one of the constants of Baudelairian religiosity—the affirmation of the expiatory nature of suffering—opens out in consciousness of divine pardon and of the plan of salvation for the world. Prayer is not then only a desperate postulation, an "ardent sob" which would die on the brink of eternal indifference. Did Baudelaire know this admirable text of Swedenborg: "If we struggle to the limit of our strength, there wafts over us a superior spirit, animating us with a superhuman power and elevating us toward a condition equivalent to the state of freedom that we have lost. For there appears to exist a divine law, according to which our will awakens the will of God" (*Œconomia Regni Animalis*). In any case he would have liked this statement which defines so well the power of attraction that prayer has—a divine magnet. Perhaps he would have lent it a sense less spiritual than magic that many a text of *Fusées* adopts: "There is in prayer a magical operation. Prayer is one of the great forces of intellectual dynamics. There is in it something like an electric recurrence" (*J.I.*, 25). One already finds this magical conception of "sustained prayer," the accumulator of strength, in the *Paradis Artificiels*, an essential book in the spiritual itinerary of the poet. One finds it again, this time transferred from the magical plane to the psychic plane, among the notes of *Mon coeur mis à nu*, where Baudelaire reveals himself completely.

> Obsession, Possession, Prayer and Faith. Moral dynamics of Jesus. Renan thinks it ridiculous that Jesus believes in the omnipotence, even material omnipotence, of Prayer and Faith. The sacraments are the means of these dynamics (*J.I.*, 101).

Concerning these formulas and others more equivocal, where amulets and sacraments go hand in hand, it would be imprudent to conclude that prayer is for the poet only a kind of magic. To speak as a poet of the "evocatory sorcery" of words is one thing, to confuse prayer and incantation is another. Baudelaire was psychologically too aware not to distinguish on the one hand the effectiveness of repeated prayer, which shapes psychic habits, and on the other hand the modification of the mind that the formula produces by its authoritarianism. It is certain that he expected an autosuggestion from it. In the religious domain as in many others, his procrastination played tricks on him. Does he not speak, in the same breath, of prayer and work: "Work, a progressive and accumulative force, bearing interest like capital itself would, in the faculties as well as in the results" (*J.I.*, 25). More than magical supersitition, the psychological repetition marks in fact the limits of prayer such as Baudelaire conceived it and no doubt practiced it. It is a method of suggestion to carry him to God, and not the direct appeal to God himself. It enters into the categories *Hygiene, Morality, Conduct, Method,* to which Baudelaire, incapable of giving form for himself, turns to conforming. Or else he seems to prescribe for himself a treatment in the hope of regenerating his strength—a hope which has only a distant connection with Christian hope: "All is reparable. There is still time. Who knows even if the new pleasures . . . ?" But because he is his patient and his physician at the same time, he can only come back to the desperate character of this task: "Let one judge the immensity of the final effort necessary for the reparation of so many losses!" (*J.I.,* 45-46).

How he spurs himself on relentlessly, and in vain! How he expects everything from himself, who knows himself incapable of the effort that he expects! "By not being converted immediately, one risks being damned" (*J.I.,* 41). Anyway, in the prayers of the last years, a confidence and an abandon are manifested, and these are signs of a change in his relation with God. This latter, *"reservoir of all strength and of all justice"* (*J.I.,* 47), can be reached through intercessors: Baudelaire's father, Mariette,[7] Poe . . . Intercession, it is true, consistent with the "consecrated" nature that Baudelaire recognizes, but only slightly conforming to strict theology; having proclaimed Poe glorified, why does then he ask for prayer for him? "All of you who have ardently sought to discover the laws of your being, who have aspired to attain the infinite, and whose repressed feelings have had to seek a frightful relief in the wine of debauchery, pray for him. Now, his purified corporeal being swims amidst beings whose existence he had some indication of, pray for him who sees and who knows, he will intercede for us" (*Œ.P.,* I, 293). But if the intercessor, closer to the center of strength, is the accumulator who communicates it, it is first of all to God himself that Baudelaire appeals, because he is that strength, and also justice; this last aspect of divine essence is new in Baudelaire in this sense, merciful and no longer vengeful. Thus then, the "egoistic phase" is ended. The mirror of the dandy is no longer his whole world: his prayer is a memento of the living and the dead. To the consciousness which made him intractable in evil succeeds the humble recognition of his misery; the offense is finally surmounted. In the depths of his indignity, he found others, first his close acquaintances, and common men among them. And also God in his infinite profundity, "the eternal confidant in this tragedy of which each one is the hero" (*J.I.,* 99), the one about whom finally, after so much heartbreak, he can say with complete certainty: "My humiliations were the grace of God" (*J.I.,* 44).

3. A Saintly Soul?

After all is examined closely, do we know much more than at the beginning of this book about the relationship that joins Baudelaire and God to each other? By measuring it, always on the side of Baudelaire alone, as if God's reality were only that which the poet gave him, one measures the inanity of a peremptory conclusion on such a well-kept secret. In spite of his letters, his intimate journals, and the memoirs—arranged—that his contemporaries have left of him, Baudelaire remains in our eyes, behind his sorrowful personage, an essentially discrete individual. This discretion appears to be due to the extreme concentration of his mind tirelessly drawn toward essence, a concentration the entire effort for which the poet attributed to himself but that I interpret, rightly or wrongly, as the work of both a dual and a single presence, to God and from God.

One can use the word *God* in many senses, all of which God contains, like his manifestations in the very thought. With such words, major and paradoxical, the mind plays its own myth and reinvents endlessly. Baudelaire's epoch liked these games: he let himself be caught in them. Besides, orphism in all its forms is the favored dream of philosophers and poets—sometimes even the foundation of their mental schemas. The tragic mythology of the fall into multiplicity, a fall identical to the creation beginning with the unthinkable and definitive loss of an *anterior absolute,* permits on the one hand a rebellious theism, agnostic with the philosophers and satanic with the poets, and on the other hand this humanistic spiritualism for which the "divine" is saved in man the self-creator. I have attempted to show how Baudelaire shared in the universal tendency of the human spirit, generator of powerful archetypal dreams which no doubt indicate an original trauma, "forgotten" somehow in the unfathomable and sempiternal memory of the species. The myths of Paradise lost, of primordial sin, of the fall without end, figure among these dreams, that, as is characteristic of poetic nature, are interpreted ever anew. No poet of any oniric depth can escape this instinctive Platonism, nor the corollary satanism. Baudelaire is the exemplary proof of it: that is one of the reasons of his importance in the poetry of all ages.

In a certain way, God comes to men through these great myths about man driven out by God, which translate into deed the refusal of God by man. More than any other, Baudelaire took this damnation seriously, endured his own refusal. His entire life is given form by this refusal, constantly reiterated, never confirmed in a definitive fashion. It is revealing that *Les Fleurs du Mal* begins, in *Bénédiction,* with a blasphemy by the mother and ends, in *La Lune Offensée,* with a blasphemy directed toward her. The drama of the poet with God, his debate against him, begins with childhood fatality. Deprived of his mother, he wants himself damned. His whole system of fall and constraint responds to this will which becomes destiny, and which he takes for the arbitrariness of God, while his own evil god is he himself. The event in which he makes up his mind is in fact the enigmatic chart of his encounter with God. The history of all of us is nothing more: it can be read like a word with several meanings, of which a single one is the key to the enigma. That too, Baudelaire knows instinctively. If he invokes Hermes, it is not without a deep reason. It is because he is the first modern man to have set himself up spiritually as universal enigma, emptying his life of its real substance in order to substitute for it Beauty alone, ambiguous, absolute Word. Is it forcing the symbol too much to see the word of the enigma in the renunciation of the last word, in the mysterious final aphasia?[8]

We have noted that the love of God is a concept which seems foreign to Baudelaire. Did he love God? Did he feel loved by him? If he loved him, it is like the second child of the *Vocations,* because God is the distant, the incommunicable one. This absence of the sense of love in Baudelaire is not illegitimate, if not to establish its erotic origin, at least to show how it is propagated from the erotic rapport with the ensemble of spirituality. The difficulties of the poet with women, the ambivalence of his relations, constantly aggravate his sorrowful intuition of being separated, exiled: they are the representation of this exile. Baudelaire did not invent this symbology; he did not even borrow it, moreover. It is a part of the mystery of the being, at the center of which—whether one admits it or not—is sexuality. He who would see in *Les Fleurs du Mal* only a magnification of vulgar eroticism would be victim of a sad misunderstanding. If so many people do read this book erotically, it is perhaps because they perceive, each on his level, the tragic aspect of eternal Eros, that no change of behavior "demythifies." To understand and appreciate Baudelaire, it is necessary to recognize in his sexual alienation a cleavage plane of this more radical division that the fracture from the being represents, or rather of the being from itself. The erotic duel with woman—angel or vampire, inextricably coveted and hated, but a stranger even from the beginning and forever—is the double aspect, as in a sacrilegious mirror, of the sempiternal combat with God.

Baudelaire suffered—without love, or from a love entirely turned into memory—the unconsolable passion for unity. He thought this unity broken forever, and attempted to retrace it, like an archeologist of the Being, through the slightest particles of Beauty. Of Beauty in itself, exclusive of the True and the Good —they too having fallen from their hypostatic reality to the rank of fragmentary and discordant ideals. This counterreligion has only one sacrament: evocation, by virtue of beautiful form, of the impossible paradisiac perfection, incorruptible substance of the spirit. For those who know what ecstatic pleasure a single word sometimes gives, a deification by art, as aberrant as it is, appears in no way absurd. Baudelaire could relieve the burden concerning the sentiment of his fall and his horrible indifference to life only through recourse to ecstasy. In this, the magical power of regeneration and the absolute respect of oneself were restored to him—precious vestiges, gathered always by poets, of a state that they believe lost. But Baudelaire, at the end of his life, seems to know a total dereliction: his spiritual life is engulfed in the consciousness of his impotence and his indignity. The enchantment of art is broken; the now bare suffering is without limits. God above knows from what abyssal travail of suffering were born the writings of the last years in which Gide, among others, was able to read only "lamentable foolishness."

In a suffering as continuously sensitive, latent even in the expression of joy, those to whom the order of the heart is not closed see too insistent a sign for them to be satisfied to attribute it to neurosis and to challenge as a manifestation of senile decay the humble expression in which this suffering is carried out. *Failure in the dimension of existence,* according to the profound ellipsis of Marcel Légaut, is the apparent summation of a great life, the reverse of its ultimate significance. In Baudelaire, as in some others of an equal and sovereign energy, this paradox forces the intellect to bow low to it like a mystery. It is for lack of this respect that Sartre's book, in places one of the most penetrating that Baudelaire has inspired, is prejudicial to the inviolable dignity of the poet and denies an authentic life of the spirit. Even to limit oneself to the analysis of the spiritual involution of the themes beginning with the psychic fatality of the poet would be to realize in an incomplete fashion, too clinical without a doubt, the interior movement of his genius. Certainly there is genius in this superior alchemy which changes the vices of nature into elements of a destiny. Elevation from the lowest to the highest, sublimation, constitutes the true spiritual *labor,* the genesis of a life inseparable from the work—a labor all the more admirable in Baudelaire since his obsessions are formidable, and since he draws from them a universal tragedy. The creature who says *I* in *Les Fleurs du Mal* is each new reader of the work, and in him, the Man of all time. The possibility of an identification so vast and spontaneous is due in the first place to the frankness of the poet before visceral shames, linked in a reciprocal fashion to careful inquiry into the inner heaven. Heir to black libertinism, Baudelaire succeeds in reversing the tendency: in him, consciousness in evil is an upward cry.

And what a cry! One can certainly find in *Les Fleurs du Mal* all the tricks or weaknesses in detail that one would like: but no other book from the French poetic domain is supported by so profound a rhetoric. The singular beauty of the attack, the variety of the harmonic combinations, the incantatory adjustment of *assertion* in the spiritual state, the dialogue endlessly reopened *by a permanent indirect apostrophe* to some supreme inner reality, intimate in the verb and passing words: so many proofs—by the very freedom of the song—of an infallible necessity, and of an effort exerted to attain its loftiness. Of this labor, the reader has for a guarantee mere perfection in the success. "Does one reveal to him all the tatters, the make-up, the pulleys, the chains, the alterations, the spoiled proofsheets, in short, all the horrors that comprise the sanctuary of art?" (Project for the *Préface* to *Les Fleurs du Mal*). No poet up to Baudelaire had bent French verse so triumphantly to modulate its secrets in such dense order, to control such an obscure subject matter. Granting the difficulty of working among the mysteries of the heart and soul, the flexibility of the style is astonishing. One senses with what concentration, with what intentional silence it sprang forth. This powerfully articulated style, whose rythm is communicated without resistance, testifies to a creative joy still not grown cold for us. The rhythm is no less implacable, invented to awaken sorrow. It drives the sensual impression to this excess where it overturns in metaphysical anguish, in the nostalgia of its own plenitude in the instant when this latter is experienced. No studied effect in that, but an effort to reach the limits, in the desperate hope of breaking through. Baudelaire agreed to pay the price of this extreme energy, by continuously cultivating *a sensibility of the damned*. In his first project for the *Préface,* immediately after a revealing outburst concerning his art: "Elegists are rabble," this sentence appears, one of the most sacred of the Gospel: "Et verbum caro factum est" [And the word was made flesh] (*F.M.,* 210). No capital letter for *verbum:* it is a question here only of incarnating the human word with man up to the very end, of penetrating, through the verbal and rythmic rigor of the poem, the density which refuses to be articulated and shaken. But to cite that text precisely is equivalent to proclaiming the sacred character of the poetic word, such as Baudelaire conceives it. We have discussed the ambivalence of this word enough to be justified in retaining whatever validity such a claim has.

Every definition of the sacred comes up against a difficulty

concerning its very nature. This word designates in effect what
has some of the characteristics of an inviolable mystery. Mysterious, the word *sacré* is by this fact contradictory: double and one,
it signifies both *saint* and *accursed*. Baudelaire, in one and the
same reality, makes the saintliness of his word correspond to the
malediction which is linked to the poet. The idea is not new:
what is new about it is the investigation of this romantic com-
monplace by a poet who has incorporated it in himself. The
sacrificial failure of Baudelaire is the exact measure of his experience of the mystery of fall and sin. It is an *unchallengeable*
failure, a spiritual lesson whose accent commands straight away
the attention even of those who do not understand its significance. The eternal success of the work is due to the undermining
of this failure by a word which changes successively into the
substance examined and transformed. Once a certain threshold of
intensity of the word is attained, the word becomes the one who
says it, or rather the one becomes the word. The whole mystery
of the man is in his *tone*.

People have compared the tone of Baudelaire to that of the
great homilists. From *Au Lecteur* to *Un Voyage à Cythère,* from
Châtiment de l'Orgueil to *Une Martyre,* from *Une Charogne* to
Delphine et Hippolyte, there are twenty great texts, sometimes
the condemned ones, about which Baudelaire, for his defense,
could say in complete truth that they *"breathe* THE HORROR OF
EVIL" (letter to Fould, and notes for his lawyer). They are
overcast with an oratorical influx which literally projects us
toward the sacred. Corrosive and purifying, the fire of the language reveals what it consumes. It lays bare the frightful beauty
of evil, exalts in it holy suffering, strikes down the spirit in a
dazzling and desperate face-to-face encounter; for man sempiternally falls *straight in the face.* The customary gesture of this poetry reminds us of Lacordaire's word: "To the man thrown down
from all his heights, he needs, to raise himself up again, only

a deep, peaceful look upon God." With the great reformer whom
he admired and whose seat in the academy he solicited, Baudelaire shares a thirst for suffering and humiliation which drove
Lacordaire to have himself trampled underfoot, cursed, given the
scourge. Baudelaire's very life could be an illustration, involuntary only in appearance, unintentional in depth, of another sublime statement of the famous Dominican: "One must make
himself humble to obtain humility." One further point of similar-
ity: the dialectics of memory and the fall, that the poet, last of the
Platonistic line, exercises with a singular asperity, Lacordaire, in a
completely different context, inscribed in his own life. "The
world is only a shadow without substance. One is in it without
being in it. One is on Calvary with Jesus Christ."

Sin, the fall, the mortifying lucidity, redemptive suffering,
flagellation of the spirit to lift it up to its true height—these
themes evidently are Christian, these exercises in the Christian
tradition. It is from them that comes, through Neoplatonism, the
"Christian" accent of Baudelaire, *an incontestable accent for the
one who understands them in a Christian sense.* It is impossible
not to take into account the consensus of so many profound
Christians, who have recognized one of their own in Baudelaire,
and found confirmation of their faith in his poignant visions of
sinful nature, which remembers and aspires with sorrow. In an
age remarkably *stupid,* rationalistic, moralistic, and licentious,
whose atheism had the Christianity that it deserved, Baudelaire,
for a small number of intelligent people, was, in the real sense of
the word, a prophet. The vehement protestation of Villiers de
l'Isle Adam—"Baudelaire is the most powerful, and the most
unified consequently, of the desperate thinkers of this wretched
century! He strikes, he is alive, he sees! Too bad for those who do
not see!" (*Chez les Passants*)—translates, with the enthusiasm of
these few, their shame before "the laughter of those who do not
know how to respect." Baudelaire is not only an awakener in art,

but he is also a man through whom poetry seized finally its own essence. This revelation flows from another, that of the incorruptible spiritual essence inside the corrupt creature. The misunderstanding as to the full significance of this double alertness is due, and we believe that we have so demonstrated, to the nature of the sacrificial suffering that it entails, according to whether one believes this suffering redemptive in God, or only evocative of Reality irremediably lost. Summing up Lacordaire's vocation in a sentence, Father Régamey wrote that he "reminds us of the whole tradition of which he is the authentic witness, according to which, by virtue of love, God's justice calls for the voluntary sacrifice and confers upon it an *irreplaceable* efficacy." One would like to apply a similar formula to Baudelaire. His idea of the irremediable forbids it, identical to that of an abrupt justice, of an exclusive necessity of all love. Whereas it leads to salvation in Lacordaire, suffering in Baudelaire is only the somber glare of inflexible Justice, the intensity of consciousness in evil.

However, when all is said, the essentials, by means of one last contradiction, escape us again. What are we to think of Baudelaire's immense capacity for compassion, which the *Petits Poèmes en Prose* bear witness to even more than *Les Fleurs du Mal?* We know quite well that this compassion under the mask of curiosity depends on consciousness in evil and is a part of the order of the fall. But in the understanding that the poet shows with respect to old ladies, widows, poor children, the solitary, the chimerical, the insane, even though he makes a spectacle of them in order to stir up his feeling of a common downfall, the Christian thinks he recognizes the same quiver of charity that their description gives rise to. Only, the charity rests in God; compassion rests only in man, and can even be a form of revolt against God. Baudelaire's suffering is often devoid of hope to such an extent that one would be tempted to see a real image of the gulf in this universal compassion. At such moments the final prayer of *Bénédiction* comes to mind again: "—Praise be to You, O God, who send us suffering . . . ," a catalyzing text of the Christian interpretation of Baudelaire. And one is certainly obliged to admit that the Platonistic reminiscence, magnificently expressed in the last stanza, is, at least in this poem, integrated in an active relation between man and God. God *gives* suffering as a way of salvation; he *invites* the poet, this oblate of suffering, who by vocation takes it upon himself and concentrates it through the ages and worlds, to enjoy the glory of the angels that his ordeal will have earned for him. This suffering to which, in the last poem of *Les Fleurs du Mal, Recueillement,* the poet addresses himself as if to his soul, is much more so in the first text of the volume, *Bénédiction,* the cornerstone of a Church or a universal Soul, against which the gates of hell shall not prevail:

> I know that suffering is the sole nobility
> Which earth and hell shall never mar,
> And that to weave my mystic crown,
> You must tax every age and every universe.

Thus, through the intermediary of one of the most used commonplaces, of this "mystical crown" drawn from the storehouse of saintly accessories, as dusty as it is familiar to Catholics, Baudelaire introduces, spread out over two stanzas, a splendid final image restorative of the broken paradisiacal unity. He thus gives us in eight lines (but, let us not forget it, at the end of a poem beginning with a double blasphemy *of* the mother and *to* the mother) the essentials of his aesthetics and his spirituality: the true celestial gory is the original Unity, of which heroically, in the indefinite multiplicity of the fall, art persists, blessed or not by God, to gather up, to bind together, the fragments.

I have said: Baudelaire's spirituality. The poet was partial to the word, which he used in a way that often appears ambiguous.

Before ending this work, a repertory of a few Baudelairian ambiguities that I consider as fundamental, which make the work and torture its author—ambiguities that I believe congenital moreover in *all poets*—it is proper for me to consider in light of the formula of Heraclitus: "They do not understand how that which struggles with itself can be harmonized: movements in an opposite direction, like the bow and the lyre." It is in such a sense that one can say of Baudelaire that he was a spiritual individual. His devotion completely memorial to the Unity and his horror over the human condition were twins: art, paradoxically, lifted the contradictions without ceasing to affirm them. He always kept present and beyond attack, at the very heart of evil, the unalterable saintliness of the Soul, of the spiritual principle taken in itself. By a word at once realistic and transfiguring, illuminating the lower depths, he expressed the absolute exile of this Soul, the abyss on the perpendicular with Unity. These are, *de profundis,* representations of an anticipatory wait for Christian reconciliation, although in themselves they translate only despair and division. A rememberer, art cannot be called a mediator between man and his Soul; it is a substitute, at most an illusion of unity. It confirms lost grandeur, but does not restore it. Now, if this alchemy of the memory, of which suffering is the source of energy and the person of Baudelaire the alembic, doubtlessly ruined the poet physically, he was visited in the very center of the destruction. The idea finally came to him, out of an excess of misery, that a mediation was possible between God and himself: an idea of a mediatory suffering—perhaps of the Mediator. I want to believe that then precisely, in a sense quite different from the one that he had thought, Baudelaire called the angels to be witness of it (*Œ.P.,* I, 7):

> O you, be the witnesses that I have done my duty
> Like a perfect chemist and like a saintly soul.

Translator's Notes

CHAPTER I

1. T. S. Eliot's essay, "Baudelaire," is included in *Selected Essays* (New York: Harcourt, Brace & Company, Inc., 1950).

2. Armand-Jean LeBouthillier de Rancé (1626–1700), the austere Trappist abbot, friend of Bossuet and Saint-Simon.

3. Baudelaire's stepfather.

4. Pierre Emmanuel, "Baudelaire et nous." *Revue des Sciences Humaines*, 89 (1958), 153–65.

CHAPTER 2

1. The French is *Cela* and *Toi,* respectively.

2. The relation of Baudelaire's father to the church is taken up further by Jean Orcibal, "Joseph-François Baudelaire était-il prêtre?" *Revue d'Histoire Littéraire de la France,* 58 (1958), 523–27. The writer denies Ruff's claims.

3. The citation varies slightly from what Baudelaire wrote: ". . . qu'est-ce que l'enfant aime si passionnément *dans* sa mère, *dans* sa bonne, *dans* sa soeur aînée?" The italics are mine. Pierre Emmanuel has adapted the line to his own text.

4. The recent publication of some hundred letters from Baudelaire to his family provides a valuable insight into the relationship of the youth to his stepfather. See Charles Baudelaire, *Lettres inédites aux siens.* Présentées et annotées par Philippe Auserve. (Paris: Editions Bernard Grasset, 1966).

5. This part of the letter is underlined by Baudelaire.

6. An engaging and curious analysis of this dream is the subject of a study by Michel Butor, *Histoire extraordinaire. Essai sur un rêve de Baudelaire* (Paris: Gallimard, 1961).

7. The French is *vil bétail.*

8. Pierre Emmanuel cites Baudelaire as having written "l'être unique *que j'aime.*" In reality the poet wrote something quite different: "Je t'embrasse non seulement comme ma mère, mais comme l'être unique *qui m'aime"*—"the only person *who loves me."* The italics are mine.

9. Choderlos de Laclos (1741–1803), author of *Les Liaisons dangereuses.* Baudelaire's interest in this epistolary novel is reflected in "Notes sur *Les Liaisons.* . . ."

10. The French is *mannequin puissant.*

11. The phrases are underlined by Baudelaire.

12. In English in the text. The poem, preceded by this English sentence, was addressed to Madame Sabatier with no date, no signature. See the *Correspondance générale,* vol. 1, p. 262. A new and unpublished letter of May 9, 1853, sent by Baudelaire from Versailles to a friend, is discussed by Jean-François Delesalle, "La Trace de quelques documents baudelairiens." *Bulletin Baudelairien,* vol. 4, No. 2 (April 9, 1969), 7–12. The article sheds light on the probable circumstances of the poet at the time he sent this message to Madame Sabatier.

13. It is thus that Baudelaire refers to his poem, *Hymne,* which accompanied this letter.

CHAPTER 3

1. The entire passage is italicized in the *Correspondance générale.*

2. The French is *moi* and *non-moi.*

3. The French is "rêve naturel" and "songe *hiéroglyphique"* respectively.

4. Italicized as follows in the original: "Je me *tue* parce que je me crois immortel, et que *j'espère.* Baudelaire has emphasized the ideas of self-destruction and hope. This letter is dated June 30 (not June 3 as in the French text).

5. The phrase appears in English in the text.

6. See Pascal, *Pensées,* 210: "The last act is tragic, however happy all the rest of the play is; at the last a little earth is thrown upon our head, and that is the end forever."

7. The reference, of course, is to Baudelaire's activities during the Revolution of 1848.

8. The phrase is in English in the text.

9. The term is in English in the text.

10. Emerson's expression appears in English in the text.

11. In Byron's own words, "The mind which is immortal makes itself/ Requital for its good or evil thoughts—/Is its own origin of ill and end" (A. III, sc. 4).

CHAPTER 4

1. Alphonse Legros (1837–1911), whose painting, *L'Angélus,* is discussed by Baudelaire in the *Salon de 1859.*

2. *Compère Mathieu* is the title of an immensely popular satirical novel by the Abbé Henri-Joseph Dulaurens, 1765.

3. Luke 2:3 reads: "And all went to be taxed, every one into his own city."

4. One of the two sections in Baudelaire's *Journaux Intimes.*

5. A follower of the radical François-Noël Babeuf (1760–1796). Babeuf claimed as his goal absolute equality for all men.

6. In English in the text.

7. Mariette, of course, is the family servant, who died sometime before 1857 and whose memory Baudelaire preserves with devotion in the poem "La servante au grand coeur. . . ." Although she is not named in the poem, the poet does refer specifically to her in his correspondence on one occasion and twice in his *Journaux Intimes.* The passage referred to here by Pierre Emmanuel is worth citing in its entirety in case there should be some readers who are unfamiliar with it. It occurs in part XXI of the section called *Fusées* where Baudelaire is outlining to himself certain principles of spiritual conduct that he feels he must adhere to: "I must offer every morning *prayer to God, that reservoir of all strength and of all justice, to my father, to Mariette and to Poe,* as intercessors."

8. It is said that Baudelaire, near the end, could utter only the syllables "Crénom," thought to represent his effort to say the blasphemous "Sacré nom de Dieu!"

Bibliography

I. WORKS

Editions of Baudelaire used for this book:
Œuvres Complètes in 18 volumes, edited by Jacques Crépet and Claude
  Pichois. Paris: Louis Conard.
Journaux Intimes, edited by J. Crépet and G. Blin. Paris: Corti, 1949.
Les Fleurs du Mal, edited by J. Crépet and G. Blin. Paris: Corti, 1942.

II. CRITICAL STUDIES

Arnold, Paul. *Le Dieu de Baudelaire.* Paris: Savel, 1947.
Asselineau, Charles. *Charles Baudelaire et son œuvre.* Paris: Nizet.
Aurevilly, Barbey d'. *Le XIXᵉ siècle,* vol. I. Paris: Mercure de France, 1964.
Bandy, W. T., and Claude Pichois. *Baudelaire devant ses contemporains.*
  Monaco: Editions du Rocher, 1957.
Bénouville, Guillain de. *Baudelaire le trop chrétien.* Paris: Grasset, 1936.
Blin, Georges. *Baudelaire.* Paris: Gallimard, 1939.
———. *Le Sadisme de Baudelaire.* Paris: Corti, 1947.
Bonnefoy, Yves. *L'Improbable.* Paris: Mercure de France, 1959.
Bourget, Paul. *Essais de Psychologie contemporaine.* Paris: Lemerre, 1885.
Chapelan, Maurice. "Baudelaire et Pascal." *Revue de France,* November
  1933, 71–100.
Daudet, Léon. *Les Pèlerins d'Emmaüs.* Paris: Grasset, 1928.
Du Bos, Charles. *Approximations.* Paris: Fayard, 1965. [Contains reprint
  of Du Bos' "Introduction à *Mon Coeur mis à nu*" and "Méditation sur
  la vie de Baudelaire."]
Eigeldinger, Marc. *Le Platonisme de Baudelaire.* Neuchâtel: La Baconnière,
  1951.
Eliot, T. S. *Essais choisis.* Paris: Éditions du Seuil, 1950.
Ferran, André. *L'Esthétique de Baudelaire.* Paris: Hachette, 1933.
Feuillerat, Albert. *Baudelaire et sa mère.* Montréal: Variétés, 1944.

Fondane, Benjamin. *Baudelaire et l'expérience du gouffre*. Paris: Seghers, 1944.

Fumet, Stanislas. *Notre Baudelaire*. Paris: Plon-Nourrit, 1926.

Hoog, Armand. *Littérature en Silésie*. Paris: Grasset, 1944.

Hubert, J. D. *L'Esthétique des Fleurs du Mal*. Paris: Cailler, 1953.

Jouve, Pierre Jean. *Le Tombeau de Baudelaire*. Neuchâtel: La Baconnière, 1942.

——— *Choix de textes de Baudelaire*. Paris: LUF.

——— *Apologie du poète*. Paris: GLM, 1947.

Keller, Luzius. *Piranèse et les poètes français*. Paris: Corti, 1966.

Kemp, Friedhelm. *Baudelaire und das Christentum*. Paris: Marburger Beiträgez. Romanischen Philologie, H. Michaelis Braun, 1939.

Laforgue, Dr. René. *L'Échec de Baudelaire*. Paris: Denoël, 1931.

Lamm, Martin. *Swedenborg*. Paris: Stock, 1936.

Maturin, Révérend. *Bertram*. Edited by Marcel Ruff. Paris: Corti, 1955.

Massin, Jean. *Baudelaire entre Dieu et Satan*. Paris: Julliard, 1945.

Milner, Max. *Le Diable dans la littérature française*, 2 vols. Paris: Corti, 1960.

Peyre, Henri. *Connaissance de Baudelaire*. Paris: Corti, 1951.

Pia, Pascal. *Baudelaire par lui-même*. Paris: Éditions du Seuil, 1952.

Pommier, Jean. *La Mystique de Baudelaire*. Paris: Belles Lettres, 1942.

Porché, François. *Baudelaire*. Paris: Flammarion, 1944.

Prévost, Jean. *Baudelaire*. Paris: Mercure de France, 1953.

Quinn, Patrick F. *The French Face of E. A. Poe*. Carbondale: Southern Illinois University Press, 1963.

Ramnoux, Clémence. *La Nuit et les Enfants de la Nuit*. Paris: Flammarion, 1959.

Raymond, Marcel. *Choix de lettres de Baudelaire*. Lausanne: Guilde du Livre, 1964.

Raynaud, Ernest. *Baudelaire et la religion du dandysme*. Paris: Mercure de France, 1918.

Régamey, R. P. *Portrait spirituel du chrétien*. Paris: Cerf, 1963.

Richard, J. P. *Poésie et Profondeur*. Paris: Editions du Seuil, 1955.

Ruff, Marcel. *L'Esprit du mal et l'esthétique baudelairienne*. Paris: Colin, 1955.

——— *Baudelaire*. Paris: Hatier, 1957.

Sartre, J. P. *Baudelaire*. Paris: Gallimard.

Starkie, Enid. *Baudelaire*. London: Faber and Faber, 1957.

Swedenborg. *Heaven and Hell*. New York: Swedenborg Foundation.

Swedenborg. *The Divine Providence*. New York: Swedenborg Foundation.

Turnell, Martin. *Baudelaire*. London: Hamish Hamilton, 1953.

Vivier, Robert. *L'Originalité de Baudelaire*. Brussels: Palais des Académies, 1965.

Vouga, Daniel. *Baudelaire et Joseph de Maistre*. Paris: Corti, 1957.

The Poems by Number and Title

LES FLEURS DU MAL (1861 edition) and other poems

Index of Persons